Understanding Project Management

Understanding Project Management

A Practical Guide

Dave C. Barrett

CANADIAN
SCHOLARS
Toronto | Vancouver

Understanding Project Management: A Practical Guide
Dave C. Barrett

First published in 2018 by
Canadian Scholars, an imprint of CSP Books Inc.
425 Adelaide Street West, Suite 200
Toronto, Ontario
M5V 3C1

www.canadianscholars.ca

Library and Archives Canada Cataloguing in Publication

Barrett, Dave C., 1959-, author
    Understanding project management : a practical guide / by Dave C. Barrett. -- 1st edition.

Includes bibliographical references.
Issued in print and electronic formats.
ISBN 978-1-77338-088-9 (softcover).--ISBN 978-1-77338-089-6 (PDF).--
ISBN 978-1-77338-090-2 (EPUB)

    1. Project management--Textbooks. 2. Textbooks. I. Title.

HD69.P75B367 2018   658.4'04   C2018-902951-X
                                                 C2018-902952-8

Cover and type design by Elisabeth Springate

Printed and bound in Canada by Marquis

Dedication

To Paula, my wife, best friend, and collaborator in all things.
Your steadfast belief in me made this book possible.

CONTENTS

PREFACE

Hello and welcome to *Understanding Project Management: A Practical Guide*. This book was written for those new to the field of project management or those looking for a practical, common sense approach to managing projects.

Over the years, I've found that textbooks written for introductory project management courses are often a difficult read. They are typically written at a highly detailed level and are most appropriate for very experienced Project Managers managing large, complex projects. For most people, though, this tends to present project management as an overwhelming set of processes and documentation that is not suited for their projects. It also suggests that project management needs to be bureaucratic, time consuming, and involve a great volume of tedious documentation. Not a great first impression to make.

This text takes a different approach. Its basis is simplicity. Project management is broken down into a series of simple, common sense processes to help manage any project. It is structured around a case study that follows a moderately sized project from initiation to completion. Throughout the case study project, the relevant project management concepts, processes, and documents are specifically demonstrated. The reader can see how project management is employed from start to finish.

My project management philosophy is that every process performed and document produced must have a practical purpose that benefits the goals of the project. Ultimately, project management is about getting things done, on time and within budget, on behalf of a customer. Any processes that do not serve this purpose should not be performed.

We can apply project management not only to our jobs, but also to our lives. It is my sincere hope that the principles and processes contained in this text will bring you greater productivity, efficiency, and simplicity at work and at home.

Dave C. Barrett

ACKNOWLEDGEMENTS

This book represents the culmination of over 20 years as a project management practitioner and over 14 years teaching the subject to post-secondary students. Not long after starting my teaching career, I realized that I had a story to tell based on this experience and I needed to write a text that would explain the benefits of project management in a simple, practical way.

With this being my first venture into the world of publishing, I'm grateful for the support of the many people I've had the opportunity to work with at Canadian Scholars. Thanks to Emma Melnyk who guided the early stages of the text. I then had the opportunity to work with not one but three production editors: Karri Yano, Lizzie Di Giacomo, and Nick Hilton. All three kept things moving along on schedule (demonstrating, I'm sure, the concepts outlined in this text). A special thanks to the copy editor, Casey Gazzellone, whose edits and thoughtful questions improved the text considerably. Thanks as well to the many others who were involved at Canadian Scholars.

In preparation of the text, I consulted with a number of industry practitioners including Mike Werbowecki, Catherine Fox, Erika Lotufo, Sarah Jones, and Ted Salidas. Their input was valuable and appreciated. Thanks to the students of the Conestoga College Bachelor of Public Relations program for providing feedback from the student perspective.

And finally, I'd like to thank Paula Barrett. As an author, I'm fortunate to be married to a professional writer and Professor of Public Relations. She has been my sounding board, providing inspiration, feedback, creative ideas, and editing. A significant amount of the case study project can be credited to Paula. Her impact on the final quality of this work cannot be fully measured.

PART I

INTRODUCTION AND
THE INITIATING PHASE

In order to follow and appreciate the ongoing case study, which uses project management to successfully complete a project, a discussion of a number of introductory concepts is essential. These concepts provide a solid foundation for the processes and documents presented throughout the remainder of the text.

After covering the introductory concepts, the text describes the management of a project from start to finish. This unit includes the first stage of a project, the Initiating Phase.

1 Understanding the Project Environment

HOW TO USE THIS TEXT

This text is structured around a case study that follows a moderately sized project from initiation to completion. At each step, the relevant **project management** concepts, tools, and documents are presented and then demonstrated within the case study. To get the most from this text, it is recommended that you read each case study instalment and consider how and why the project management tools are being used. The concepts and tools of project management are less relevant in the abstract but come alive during actual projects.

Project templates are employed throughout the text as a way of demonstrating how the concepts of project management may be implemented. This should not be interpreted as a suggestion that all projects must use all the project templates exactly as written. Project management does not equate to the completion of document templates. Instead, each template should be viewed as indicating the type of thinking that should take place during the project. While you are welcome to use these templates within a project, the actual format and level of detail depend on the needs of the project. For example, when creating a project schedule, the actual format may be activities listed on a whiteboard, in a spreadsheet, or in project management software. What is most important is the thinking and actions that take place, rather than the format of the documents.

WHAT IS A PROJECT?

When setting out to study the field of project management, a key question is: what is it that makes something a project? While there are many characteristics that projects tend to share, there are two conditions that are fundamental and therefore must be present:

- The project is temporary—there is a beginning and an end.
- The outcome of the project is unique—that is, different in some way from anything else produced.

The **Project Management Institute** (2013) provides the following definition of a **project**: "a temporary endeavour undertaken to create a unique product, service, or result."[1]

Non-project work is known as **operations**. Operations involve the ongoing creation of the goods or services of an organization. Examples of operations include the production facility of a car company or the call centre of an insurance company.

Within organizations, projects are initiated in order to create something new or to implement change. This could be an updated product design, a marketing campaign, or a revamp of the company's website. When projects are completed, the finished product, service, or results are transferred to the operations of the company.

As every project is unique, projects vary in their scope, duration, and complexity. The requirements of the project can be well known and stable, or unknown and volatile.

Projects may also vary significantly in size. For example, for an insurance company call centre department:

- A small project could involve a review of recently completed calls in order to recommend changes to the phone scripts used by the Customer Service Representatives.
- A medium project could involve an upgrade of computer software to improve the call centre's automatic call routing.
- A large project could involve a relocation of the call centre to another city.

WHAT IS PROJECT MANAGEMENT?

Given the definition of projects as temporary and unique activities, the next question is how best to manage them. The use of project management promotes an orderly progression from the start to the end of the project. It involves the use of various processes and documents to effectively plan and execute the project. The Project Management Institute (2013) defines project management as "the application of knowledge, skills, tools, and techniques to project activities to meet the project requirements."[2]

Project management comes in many forms. It may refer to a profession (i.e., the project management profession), it may refer to a job title (i.e., a Project Manager), or it may refer to an activity (e.g., the Marketing Manager performs a number of project management activities). Some organizations may perform project management with strict adherence to formal processes while other organizations may use informal processes.

Each form of project management described above may be appropriate for certain organizations and projects. As projects may vary in terms of their scope, duration, and complexity, it can be challenging to determine the appropriate amount of project management processes to use. For example, if an insufficient amount of project management is used, the project may underperform due to a lack of planning and control. However, if too much project management is used, the project may be burdened with an unnecessary amount of process. Understanding the characteristics of the project and then determining the appropriate amount of project management required is an important decision for the Project Manager to make.

Introduction to the Case Study

Deco Productions is a medium-sized software company located in the Midwest that employs over 300 people. Casey Serrador founded the company in 2006. As an avid photographer, Casey guides the company in the development of software related to photography and video production. The company name was inspired by Casey's interest in the Art Deco period. She was drawn to the streamlined forms and smooth lines inherent in the period and looks to instill this modern elegance into the culture and products of her company. The Art Deco period's focus on technological and social progress is also a high priority for Deco Productions.

The company's goal is simple: to provide industry-leading, quality products and services to its customers. This best in class strategy requires a culture of constant innovation with frequent product updates in order to stay ahead of the competition.

Deco Productions promotes an open and collaborative environment. Work hours are flexible and many employees spend time both in the office and working from home. The office has an open concept design with a few private rooms reserved for customer meetings and private conversations.

Casey's philosophy is that people make better decisions when they have a stake in the outcomes of the organization. This is accomplished through an employee profit-sharing program. She also believes that the people closest to the work are best able to understand how the work should be performed. Employees and teams are empowered to modify their own processes in order to improve the company's performance.

Town hall meetings are held on a monthly basis where Casey and her management team describe the company's recent progress and upcoming challenges. Employees have the opportunity to ask questions and provide ideas. There are numerous instances where ideas raised during the meeting were subsequently implemented to the benefit of the company.

Deco Productions develops camera and video software for the following markets:

- Consumers (mobile device camera applications)
- Camera manufacturers
- Video camera manufacturers

One of Deco Productions' software products is DecoCam. DecoCam is an industry-leading software application for the mobile device market. Consumers are able to purchase and download the product to their mobile devices. The product employs state-of-the-art technology to produce digital pictures with superior colour and clarity.

A new version of DecoCam (Version 4) has been proposed. This version would introduce a new feature known as the Photo Assistant. This feature would perform as follows:

- Before taking a picture, the user would have the option of selecting the Photo Assistant.
- The user is prompted to take a short video of up to 10 seconds of the immediate surroundings.
- The Photo Assistant analyzes the video and recommends an optimal setting in terms of the direction, angle, and content of the picture.

While the initial estimate to create this feature is high, it is expected that it will be popular with consumers and help ensure DecoCam maintains its position as a market leader. Though this initiative has not yet been approved, many in the organization are hopeful that the project will commence shortly.

THE PROJECT LIFE CYCLE

As indicated earlier in this chapter, projects produce a product, service, or result. The question then becomes how best to organize the activities needed to complete the project. What follows is a basic process for creating something new:

1. Determine the overall parameters of the project, such as why this project should be performed, when it needs to be completed, and what funds are available to complete the project.
2. Plan the details of the work to be performed including what will be produced, when it will be completed, and the resulting cost.

3. Produce the product, service, or result based on the planning.
4. End the project, comparing the results achieved to the original parameters of the project.

Each of the above steps is represented by a project **phase**. The collection of phases representing the entire project is known as the **Project Life Cycle** (PLC). The PLC used in this text is as follows:

- Initiating
- Planning
- Executing
- Closing

Each phase represents a time period of the project when similar activities take place. Project phases are advantageous as they provide clarity to the project team regarding the type of activities required during each time period. The end of a project phase is often used as a review point to assess whether the project should continue. For example, at the end of the Initiating Phase, a decision may be made regarding whether the project should proceed to the Planning Phase.

The following PLC will be followed throughout the first four parts of this text as demonstrated in the diagram below. This form of project management is often called the traditional waterfall method. The waterfall terminology comes from the idea that the work flows from one phase to the next much like a waterfall flows downwards from one level to the next.

A Practical Guide to the Project Life Cycle

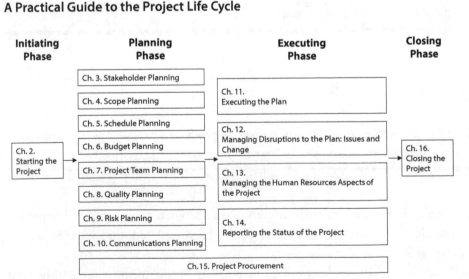

Different organizations and projects may use other names for each phase or contain a different number of phases. For example, for systems development projects, planning is often replaced by analysis and design. On other projects, executing may be known as implementation, development, or construction.

The width of the phases in the above diagram is not representative of the duration or the amount of work required. Instead, the Initiating and Closing Phases are normally very brief and require a minimum of resources. Increased time and resources are required during the Planning and Executing Phases.

PROJECT STAKEHOLDERS

Projects are not performed in isolation but instead involve or impact individuals, groups, and organizations known as **project stakeholders**. Project stakeholders may be internal or external to the project's company.

It is important to identify and manage the relationship with the project stakeholders as they may positively or negatively impact the project's outcomes.

Project stakeholders typically present during projects include:
- Project Sponsor
- Project Manager
- Project Team
- Customers
- Managers
- Suppliers
- Government

Two key project stakeholders that are required for every project are the Project Sponsor and Project Manager. The Project Sponsor provides the funding for the project. While a Project Sponsor does not actively manage the project, they provide overall guidance and approve major decisions during the project. The Project Manager's function is to actively manage the project, ideally using sound project management principles.

PROCESS GROUPS

Related to project phases is the concept of **process groups**. The Project Management Institute (2013) has grouped the processes of project management into five distinct groups:
- Initiating Process Group
- Planning Process Group
- Executing Process Group
- Closing Process Group
- Monitoring and Controlling Process Group[3]

Note that the first four process groups have the same names as the four project phases of the PLC previously discussed. They are related as follows:

Process Groups and Project Phases

Processes from the:	Take place primarily during the:
Initiating Process Group	Initiating Phase
Planning Process Group	Planning Phase
Executing Process Group	Executing Phase
Closing Process Group	Closing Phase
Monitoring and Controlling Process Group	All phases

PROJECT CONSTRAINTS

While customers would ideally prefer that a project produces as much as possible, there are limitations to what can be achieved. These limitations are known as **project constraints**.

The three fundamental project constraints, often referred to as the triple constraint, are:
- Scope: the features and characteristics of the final project
- Time: the amount of time available to complete the project
- Cost: the budget available to complete the project

The Triple Constraint

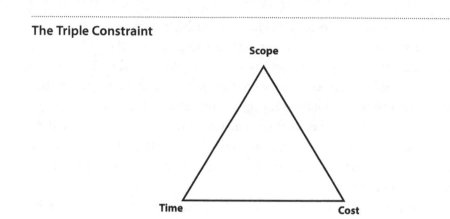

The triangle diagram above clearly displays the relationship between the constraints. Each constraint is connected to the other two constraints. The challenge for the Project Manager is to deliver the results of the project while satisfying each of the project constraints. In other words, they must deliver the required scope by the due date and stay within the budget. The difficulty occurs when one (or more) of the constraints are exceeded. For example, if additional features are required, this may also affect the time constraint (it may take longer) and the cost constraint (the budget may be exceeded).

Over time, additional constraints have been recognized and added to the original three constraints:

- Quality: the level of quality required for the project
- Resources: the availability of people, material, and equipment to complete the project
- Risk: the level of risk that is present for the project

Six Project Constraints

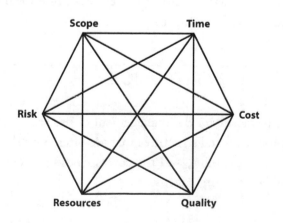

The hexagon displays the more complex relationship between the six project constraints. As shown, each of the constraints may impact the other five.

For example, let's say that a project is already underway when it becomes apparent that the project's target date may not be met. Rather than delaying the project, the Project Manager looks at the following options:

- Overtime could be scheduled or additional workers could be added to the project. However, this tends to increase the costs of the project (that is, it affects the cost constraint), and additional workers may not be available (resource constraint).
- The workers could attempt to work faster and get more work done in the remaining time. However, this tends to cause problems (quality constraint) and may damage the reputation of the organization (risk constraint).
- A discussion could be held with the project sponsors in order to reduce the results of the project (scope constraint).

This example demonstrates an important characteristic of constraints: when one constraint changes, it often impacts many if not all of the other constraints. One would hope that changes to constraints would be a rare event on a project. Unfortunately, they are relatively common. During projects, budgets often change, schedules change, resources are unavailable or delayed, changes to the scope of the project are proposed, and so on. Managing the interaction between project constraints becomes an ongoing task.

The challenge for the Project Manager is to determine the best course of action to take when constraints occur. The Project Manager must balance the satisfaction of the customer with the performance of the project. Excellent communication and diplomacy skills are required in order to arrive at an acceptable solution. A Project Manager's skill in these areas often means the difference between the success and failure of the project.

PROGRAMS AND PORTFOLIOS

This text focuses primarily on the management of projects. However, there are two additional project-related structures that are often present within organizations: programs and portfolios, and the corresponding disciplines of program management and portfolio management.

When a number of projects in an organization share a common business objective, it is often useful to group them together in order to coordinate their activities. This collection of projects is known as a **program** and is managed by a Program Manager. The Project Manager of each project within the program works under the direction of the Program Manager. A key benefit of program management is to increase the effectiveness of coordination between projects in areas such as:

- coordinating decisions across projects;
- coordinating schedules of projects;
- coordinating resources across projects.

For most organizations, there are usually a significant number of possible projects and programs that the organization may undertake. However, due to financial and resource constraints, organizations must choose a subset of these initiatives to perform at any one time in order to achieve the strategic objectives of the organization. This subset of projects and programs is known as the organization's project **portfolio.** The process of managing the content of the portfolio, including adding, prioritizing, and removing its projects and programs, is called portfolio management. A Portfolio Manager is a senior role within an organization due to the strategic nature of the work involved.

Case Study Update: Programs and Portfolios

Casey Serrador takes her place at the head of the boardroom table. It is 8:55 a.m. and almost time for the monthly senior management strategy meeting to begin. Casey's senior management team, the heads of each division within Deco Productions, attend the meeting.

After a review of the company strategy and a discussion of Casey's recent interview on a business cable news special, the agenda turns to the selection of the next major company initiative. There are three possibilities:

1. An update to Deco Productions' suite of video camera software that has been recently requested by one of Deco Productions' key customers (a major video camera manufacturer).

2. The creation of a completely new service that would allow DecoCam customers to upload pictures to a system that would automatically create physical books, such as yearbooks or vacation albums.

3. An update to the DecoCam application that would introduce the Photo Assistant feature.

Continued

Each initiative is presented by a different executive, who outlines both the strategic benefits and the likely costs to be incurred.

Jackson Woodhouse, Vice-President, Customer Support, presents the first option. Most of the discussion revolves around the strategic importance of the customer and the likelihood that they could be lost to one of Deco Productions' competitors if the project is not completed.

Brittany Bianchi, Vice-President, Product Development, presents the second option. Concerns are raised that other companies already provide the proposed functionality and that it doesn't differentiate Deco Productions in any significant way.

Arun Singh, Vice-President, Mobile Products Distribution, presents the third option. The possible development of the Photo Assistant feature generates a great deal of discussion. While the feature is bold and unique, the costs are also projected to be high. If the project fails, it would cause a significant hit to the company's bottom line.

After a period of discussion, the decision becomes clear. Casey summarizes the discussion by confirming that the DecoCam Version 4 project containing the Photo Assistant application will be starting soon. As part of the discussion, a goal for DecoCam V4 is defined: a 5% increase in the mobile camera software market share.

The executive team then shifts its focus to how best to organize this initiative. After a further period of discussion, the DecoCam V4 Program is created consisting of the following projects:

- DecoCam V4 Development
- DecoCam V4 Installation
- DecoCam V4 Technical Writing
- DecoCam V4 Product Launch

Each member of the management team considers how this new program impacts their area of responsibility. Arun Singh looks at the list of projects. The DecoCam V4 Product Launch project will be performed within his department. He makes a mental note to get a Project Manager assigned to this project as soon as possible.

CHAPTER SUMMARY

Key Concepts

1. A project is defined as a temporary endeavour undertaken to create a unique product, service, or result.
2. Project management is defined as the application of knowledge, skills, tools, and techniques to project activities to meet the project requirements.

3. The Project Life Cycle (PLC) consists of the following four phases: Initiating, Planning, Executing, and Closing.

4. Project stakeholders are individuals, groups, and organizations that are involved in, or impacted by, a project.

5. The processes of a project are organized into five project management process groups: Initiating, Planning, Executing, Closing, and Monitoring and Controlling.

6. The six project constraints are: scope, time, cost, quality, resources, and risk.

7. Programs are groups of projects that share a common business objective.

8. Portfolios are the project initiatives selected by an organization to perform in order to achieve the strategic objectives of the organization.

Key Terminology

Operations: The area responsible for the ongoing creation of the goods or services of an organization.

Phase: A time period of the project when similar activities take place.

Portfolio: The collection of projects and programs that the organization actively manages in order to achieve its strategic objectives.

Process Group: A group of similar or complementary project management processes. The five process groups are initiating, planning, executing, monitoring and controlling, and closing.

Program: A number of projects that are related in some way, such as a common business objective.

Project: A temporary endeavour undertaken to create a unique product, service, or result.

Project Constraints: Limits to what a project is able to achieve. The six project constraints are scope, time, cost, quality, resources, and risk.

Project Life Cycle: A collection of project phases that represents the entire project.

Project Management: The application of knowledge, skills, tools, and techniques to project activities to meet the project requirements.

Project Management Institute: A global professional organization that defines standards and guidelines for the project management field.

Project Stakeholders: Individuals or groups who have some involvement or are affected in some way by the project.

DISCUSSION QUESTIONS

1. Create a list of projects from your personal experience. Do they all meet the criteria of being temporary and unique? What other attributes do they share?

2.   What personal traits would be helpful for someone managing a project? What personal traits would be helpful for someone managing the operations of an organization? What are the similarities and differences between the two roles?

3.   Perform an online search to research the history of project management. Based on your findings, what factors led to the development of project management?

4.   What is the difference between the Planning Process Group and the Planning Phase?

5.   Think of an example from your personal, work, or school activities where a change in one constraint caused an impact to one or more other constraints. Describe the example.

6.   Create a list of the possible personal projects that you could potentially undertake over the next two years. How will you determine which of the projects you will perform?

NOTES

1.   Project Management Institute. (2013). *A Guide to the Project Management Body of Knowledge (PMBOK® Guide)* (5th ed.), p. 3. Newtown Square, PA.

2.   Project Management Institute. (2013). *A Guide to the Project Management Body of Knowledge (PMBOK® Guide)* (5th ed.), p. 5. Newtown Square, PA.

3.   Project Management Institute. (2013). *A Guide to the Project Management Body of Knowledge (PMBOK® Guide)* (5th ed.), p. 5. Newtown Square, PA.

2 Starting the Project

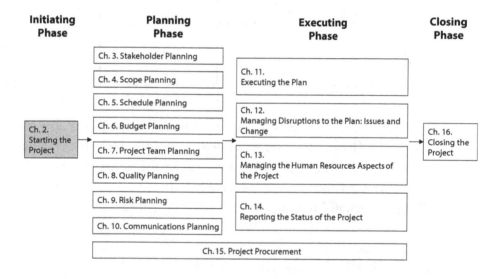

Initiating Phase	Planning Phase	Executing Phase	Closing Phase
Ch. 2. Starting the Project	Ch. 3. Stakeholder Planning	Ch. 11. Executing the Plan	Ch. 16. Closing the Project
	Ch. 4. Scope Planning		
	Ch. 5. Schedule Planning	Ch. 12. Managing Disruptions to the Plan: Issues and Change	
	Ch. 6. Budget Planning		
	Ch. 7. Project Team Planning	Ch. 13. Managing the Human Resources Aspects of the Project	
	Ch. 8. Quality Planning		
	Ch. 9. Risk Planning	Ch. 14. Reporting the Status of the Project	
	Ch. 10. Communications Planning		
	Ch. 15. Project Procurement		

INTRODUCTION TO STARTING THE PROJECT

In the previous chapter, the DecoCam V4 Program was defined as consisting of four projects. The remainder of this case study will focus on one of the projects: the DecoCam V4 Product Launch.

This chapter describes the activities that take place during the first phase of the PLC: the Initiating Phase. While it is a relatively short phase, it is very important that it is completed effectively. The Initiating Phase provides the foundation for the remainder of the project.

There are two main steps when starting the project:

Starting the Project

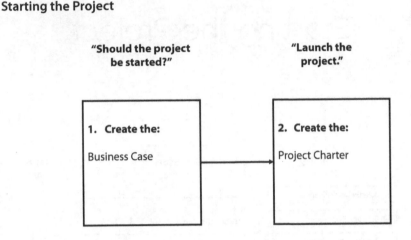

The first step involves determining the feasibility of the project and results in the creation of the **Business Case**. Assuming the project moves forward, the next step is to set the overall goals and objectives of the project through the creation of the **Project Charter**. The project should then be officially launched through a **Project Kickoff Meeting** with key project participants.

SHOULD THE PROJECT BE STARTED?

When starting a project, there are often a number of broad options to consider for how the project may be implemented or even whether the project should be performed at all. Determining the options and selecting the best course of action is known as creating the Business Case. The advantage of this process is that it provides a clear direction and focus for the project.

When creating the Business Case, the likely costs are compared to the potential benefits. Estimated costs may be tangible (e.g., labour costs) or intangible (e.g., increased risk of missing a deadline). Benefits may be tangible (e.g., increased sales) or intangible (e.g., increased brand recognition).

The completion of a Business Case provides the management of the organization with the information necessary to determine the best course of action when initiating the project. The senior management of the organization is typically responsible for the final approval of the recommended option, as it may result in significant resources being spent and it could impact other initiatives within the organization.

The following is the Business Case report template:

Business Case Template

BUSINESS CASE	
Proposed Project	[At this point, the project is not yet approved, so it may not have its final name or the name may change. The current name or identifier should be included here.]
Date Produced	[The date the Business Case is produced.]
Background	[This section should include information that will help the reader understand the context and background history regarding the potential project. This section should not be written assuming that the background is common knowledge, but instead should be specific in order to create a common understanding of the context.]
Business Need/ Opportunity	[This section should demonstrate the business need or opportunity that the proposed project will address.]
Options	[This section documents the potential approaches to complete the project. There is always a minimum of two options: perform the project or do nothing.]

Cost-Benefit Analysis

[This section contains the detailed costs and benefits of each option listed in the previous section. The costs may include considerations such as financial expenditures, the amount of time required, possible risks, and the potential for reduced quality. The benefits may include the potential of increased sales, market share, and brand recognition, and the reduction of errors and ongoing costs. Each option should be clearly identified and listed separately.]

Recommendation

[This section contains the recommended option from the previous section.]

Case Study Update: Creating the Business Case

Working late on a Friday afternoon, Sophie Featherstone is updating the final project documents for a recently completed project. Sophie has been with Deco Productions for just over two years, working as a Senior Project Manager in the Product Distribution department.

As she packs up to leave, her phone rings. Checking the call display, she sees that it is Arun Singh, Vice-President, Mobile Products Distribution.

"Hello, Sophie. Glad you're still here," says Arun. "I need you to manage the product launch for the new version of DecoCam. This is the biggest update to DecoCam that we've had. Its goal is a 5% increase in market share, so there is a lot riding on this one. Given all the good work you've done over the last couple of years, I know you're up to it."

Continued

Sophie replies, "Sounds great, Arun. It will be great to work with you again."

Hanging up the phone, Sophie pulls out her notebook and starts a to-do list. She has a lot of work to do to get this project up and running quickly.

There are usually many different options for completing a project. On a notepad, she sketches three main options:

A. Soft product launch: consisting of minimal promotional activities that would rely primarily upon word-of-mouth from the existing DecoCam users.

B. Moderate product launch: consisting of option A plus promotions through the company's existing communication channels.

C. Full product launch: consisting of option B plus the development of a promotional video and creation of trade show materials.

Over the next few days, Sophie consults with a number of people within the company. This helps her define the high-level content and develop a reasonable estimate for each option.

As she completes her work, one of the options emerges as the best choice and it becomes clear what her recommendation will be. She books a meeting with the Project Sponsor, Arun, who will select the final option.

The following is the resulting Business Case developed during the case study project:

Business Case

BUSINESS CASE	
Proposed Project	DecoCam V4 Product Launch
Date Produced	March 2, 2020
Background	Deco Productions is updating its DecoCam product to include a new feature known as the Photo Assistant. The subject of this business case is the work involved to launch this new product.
Business Need/ Opportunity	DecoCam is currently the leading camera-related application in the mobile market and it is important that this leadership position is maintained. An effective launch of the new version of DecoCam will positively impact the sales of the new product leading to increased revenues and market share of this product. An important objective of this project is that it must be ready to launch once the development of the new product is complete.

Options	The following are the high-level options:
	A. Soft product launch
	   • Product information would be updated on the company website and printed materials, but otherwise no additional promotional activities would take place.
	B. Moderate product launch
	   • This would include Option A along with promotional activities using the company's existing communication channels.
	C. Full product launch
	   • This would include Option B along with a promotional video and the creation of trade show materials.

Cost-Benefit Analysis

Option A—Soft product launch
Costs
• Budget: $10,000
• Possibility of delaying the product launch date: 1%
Benefits
• Market share: estimated that DecoCam will maintain its current market share

Option B—Moderate product launch
Costs
• Budget: $25,000
• Possibility of delaying the product launch date: 5%
Benefits
• Market share: estimated that DecoCam will increase its current market share by 3% within one year of the product launch
• Brand recognition: moderate increase in the recognition of Deco Productions as a provider of high-quality photography and video-related products

Option C—Full product launch
Costs
• Budget: $60,000
• Possibility of delaying the product launch date: 10%
Benefits
• Market share: estimated that DecoCam will increase its current market share by 6% within one year of the product launch
• Brand recognition: significant increase in the recognition of Deco Productions as a provider of high-quality photography and video-related products

Recommendation

Given the potential for increased market share and brand recognition, Option C (full product launch) is recommended.

LAUNCH THE PROJECT

With the work and decisions that have been completed to this point, the next step is to officially launch the project by creating the Project Charter. Creation of the Project Charter signals that the project has started and authorizes the

Project Manager to proceed with the project. The creation of a Project Charter is also used to ensure that there is agreement between the Project Sponsor, Project Manager, and other key stakeholders. The Project Charter will typically contain information such as the:

- *Project Goals and Objectives*: Project goals define the destination of the project—that is, what the project will achieve and how it will support the goals of the organization. Goals should be specific and measurable. Objectives are the specific outcomes that are required in order to meet the project goals.
- *Project Budget*: The budget represents the funds that are available for the project. The amount may be based on initial estimates performed during the Initiating Phase or may represent the amount that was originally allocated for the project.
- **Project Sponsor and Project Manager**: The Project Sponsor and Project Manager are two important roles required in order to proceed with the project.
- *Additional Key Project Stakeholders*: During the Initiating Phase, project stakeholders are identified. Those stakeholders who will be actively involved in the project and play a significant role are listed in the Project Charter.
- *Overall project **milestones***: Significant points in the project, known as milestones, are listed in the Project Charter. Examples of overall milestones are the start of the project and the target date for the completion of the project.
- *Overall Project Risks*: Any risks (i.e., unexpected events that could affect the outcome of the project) known at this point in the project should be listed in the Project Charter.

The following is the Project Charter template:

Project Charter Template

PROJECT CHARTER	
Project Name	[This section contains the project name that should appear consistently on all project documents. Organizations often have project naming conventions.]
Date Produced	[The date the Project Charter is produced.]

Project Goals	[This section defines what the project will achieve and how it supports the goals of the organization.]
Project Objectives	[This section defines the specific outcomes that are required to achieve the project goals.]
Project Budget	[This section contains the funds available for the project.]
Project Sponsor	[Name of project sponsor and job title.]
Project Manager	[Name of project manager and job title.]

Additional Key Project Stakeholders

[The names of key stakeholders that are known at this point in the project, including their job title or project role.]

Overall Project Milestones	Dates
[A list of the key milestones that are known at this point in the project.]	[Milestone dates.]

Overall Project Risks

[A list of the overall risks that are known at this point in the project.]

Case Study Update: Creating the Project Charter

Sophie has accomplished a great deal over the last couple of weeks. The Business Case that she created was very useful for selecting the best option for the product launch. Her boss appreciated how well the options were presented and accepted her recommendation to proceed with the full product launch option.

Over the last few days, Sophie has been in various discussions with a number of stakeholders within Deco Productions, including Casey and Arun. Through these discussions, she has clarified her understanding of the project's goals and objectives, key milestones, and possible risks. The only problem is that she suspects that she is the only one who understands the big picture of the project. Additionally, Sophie is concerned that there are many people within the organization who are not aware of this project, let alone that she is the Project Manager.

She decides that it's time to summarize this information into a written report—the Project Charter. Given the number of stakeholders who will be affected by her project, she checks her calendar in order to book a Project Kickoff Meeting.

The following is the Project Charter for the case study project:

Project Charter

PROJECT CHARTER	
Project Name	DCV4Launch–DecoCam V4 Product Launch
Date Produced	March 25, 2020
Project Goals	The goals of the project are to successfully launch DecoCam V4 by the target date, within the project budget, and to support the company's goal of a 5% increase in DecoCam's market share.
Project Objectives	The objectives of the project are to: • Update the product information on the company website and printed materials. • Promote the new product through existing communication channels. • Create a promotional video. • Create tradeshow materials.
Project Budget	$60,000
Project Sponsor	Arun Singh, Vice-President, Mobile Products Distribution
Project Manager	Sophie Featherstone, Senior Project Manager

Additional Key Project Stakeholders
Casey Serrador, CEO, Deco Productions
Jackson Woodhouse, Vice-President, Customer Support
Brittany Bianchi, Vice-President, Product Development

Overall Project Milestones	Dates
Project starts	March 23, 2020
Project approval	March 25, 2020
Trade show materials complete	May 8, 2020
Project complete	May 13, 2020

Overall Project Risks
Errors are present in the product launch materials.
Delays during the project cause the product launch to be late.

The Project Kickoff Meeting

It is usually advisable for the Project Manager to schedule a Project Kickoff Meeting once the Project Charter is published. Key project stakeholders including the Project Sponsor, other senior managers, and project team members should be invited to attend. The agenda for this meeting should include the following:

- Introduction of the project stakeholders (if they have not previously met)
- Review of the organization's strategy and goals
- Discussion of the project goals, objectives, and budget
- Overview of key milestones throughout the project
- Discussion of any known risks or current issues

The desired result of this meeting is that the key stakeholders understand and support the project. The meeting should allow for any issues or concerns to be raised, as it will be more effective to address these early on rather than later in the project.

The Project Sponsor should approve the Project Charter. This can be accomplished at the Project Kickoff Meeting, if it takes place. With the completion of the Project Charter and Project Kickoff Meeting, the project is ready to enter the Planning Phase of the PLC.

CHAPTER SUMMARY

Key Concepts

1. In order for a project to start, the senior management of the sponsoring organization develops a project concept.
2. Goals and objectives are defined for the project.
3. Key project roles include the Project Sponsor and Project Manager.
4. The project officially begins when the Project Sponsor approves the Project Charter.

Key Terminology

Business Case: A documented study to determine the costs and benefits of a proposed initiative that will be used as a basis for future project work.

Milestone: An important event that occurs during a project.

Project Charter: A document that signals that the project has started and authorizes the Project Manager to proceed with the project.

Project Kickoff Meeting: A meeting held with key project stakeholders at the end of the Initiating Phase to officially launch the project.

Project Manager: The individual who is assigned to manage the project and ensure that the objectives are completed.

Project Sponsor: The individual who provides the financial resources, support, and approval for the project.

DISCUSSION QUESTIONS

1. Should a Business Case be created for every project? If yes, why should they always be performed? If no, when would a Business Case not be required?
2. Think of a home renovation project that you have either been involved in or have observed. Create a list of all of the stakeholders for this project.
3. How do project goals differ from project objectives? Do you need to define both in the Project Charter?
4. What are some of the negative outcomes that could occur if a Project Charter is not produced?
5. Is a Project Kickoff Meeting necessary? Describe the benefits of holding this meeting.
6. Perform an online search to research the challenges associated with the Initiating Phase of a project. Based on your findings, what are some problems that may occur during this phase?

PART II

THE PLANNING PHASE

With the completion of the Initiating Phase, the goals and objectives have been established and the project has officially started. The Initiating Phase should have answered the question of why the project is being performed.

The project now moves into the next phase: the Planning Phase. During this period, the details of the project are determined and the following questions are answered:

- Who will be involved or affected by the project? Who will deliver the project?
- What will the project create? What are the risks? What will it cost?
- Where will the work be performed?
- When will the work be completed?
- How will the work be performed?

The chapters related to the Planning Phase are presented in a logical order that demonstrates how the overall project plan is created in the case study. It is important to understand that this progression of planning is not a completely linear process. Decisions made in one area of planning may impact previously developed plans. For example, after defining the content of the project (scope), detailed cost planning may then require the project scope to be revisited and updated.

Each chapter's planning processes should be thought of as providing an additional component to the overall project plan. Each component can impact any or all of the previously developed plans. The components are not complete until *all* components are complete.

The creation of the project plan is important because it contains the characteristics of the project to be completed, enables decisions to be made, and is used to guide the execution of the project.

Once the project begins to be executed, real world activities and problems begin to occur. Project Managers often find themselves confronted with issues that they didn't predict during planning. The duration and cost of the actual work is often very different from what was estimated. In short, plans are often proven to be incorrect during the execution of the project.

Some may use this as a reason to eliminate the planning process. Instead, this is why planning is important. The planning process immerses the Project Manager and the project team in the details of the project, as they are required to look at it from many angles and become intimately familiar with the details. This prepares the Project Manager and project team to handle the unpredictable events that naturally occur during the execution of the project.

The challenge for the Project Manager is to determine the amount of planning that should be performed. There should be enough planning to understand the project but not an excessive amount that attempts to perfect a plan that will likely change during execution.

3 Stakeholder Planning

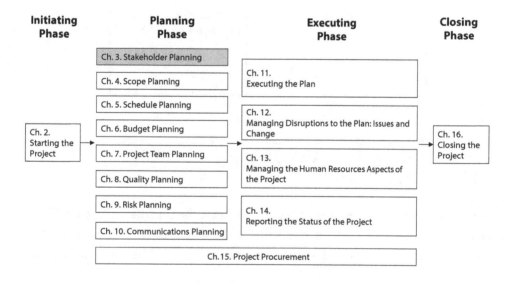

Initiating Phase	Planning Phase	Executing Phase	Closing Phase

- Ch. 3. Stakeholder Planning
- Ch. 4. Scope Planning
- Ch. 5. Schedule Planning
- Ch. 2. Starting the Project
- Ch. 6. Budget Planning
- Ch. 7. Project Team Planning
- Ch. 8. Quality Planning
- Ch. 9. Risk Planning
- Ch. 10. Communications Planning

- Ch. 11. Executing the Plan
- Ch. 12. Managing Disruptions to the Plan: Issues and Change
- Ch. 13. Managing the Human Resources Aspects of the Project
- Ch. 14. Reporting the Status of the Project

- Ch. 16. Closing the Project

Ch. 15. Project Procurement

INTRODUCTION TO STAKEHOLDER PLANNING

Before delving into the details of the project's requirements, it is useful to consider the project stakeholders who will be involved in or affected by the project.

Project stakeholders are important throughout the project. The project itself is based on project stakeholder requirements. The scope, schedule, and budget will require the appropriate stakeholder approval, and the acquisition of the project personnel often requires stakeholder negotiation and agreement. The perceived quality of the project will be based on the assessment of stakeholders.

The purpose of stakeholder planning is not only to identify all of the project's stakeholders, but also to build effective and appropriate relationships with each stakeholder.

There are two main steps when planning for project stakeholders:

Stakeholder Planning

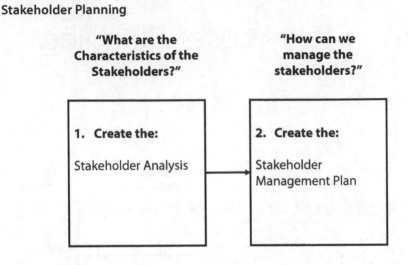

WHAT ARE THE CHARACTERISTICS OF THE STAKEHOLDERS?

The stakeholders of the project were identified during the Initiating Phase. During planning, this list is expanded as additional stakeholders are identified. Each stakeholder is reviewed to assess their level of power, interest, and support.

Level of Power

Power is the stakeholder's ability to positively or negatively affect the project. This power may come from a number of sources such as their formal job position, their role in the project, or their perceived expertise. Examples of stakeholders with high levels of power include:
- the CEO of the company (job position);
- the person managing resources for the organization (role);
- an industry expert in a field relevant to the project (perceived expertise).

Stakeholders who may have lower levels of power include:
- project team members;
- other managers in the organization;
- the general public.

The assessment of power can be difficult as it may not be readily apparent who holds power. For example, while project team members may generally possess a lower level of power, a project team member with a unique skill set would likely possess a higher level of power. Power levels may also shift over the course of a project. For example, the general public may possess a low level of power at the start of a project, but if an individual or group attracts the attention of the media, their power level may increase.

The assessment of power often requires an understanding of the internal politics that almost always exists within organizations.

Level of Interest

A stakeholder's **interest** is the level of concern or engagement that they have with the project. A stakeholder with a high level of interest is aware of and feels invested in the project, while a stakeholder with a lower level of interest is less aware of and less invested in the project. For example, Project Sponsors often possess a high level of interest regarding a project. However, if the project is very small, or if the Project Sponsor is very busy, they may have a low level of interest in the project.

As with the level of power, stakeholder interest may be difficult to assess. Using the example above, the Project Sponsor would need to be observed in order to determine their level of interest.

Level of Support

The third category for assessing stakeholders is their **level of support**, which may be supportive, neutral, or unsupportive.

The Project Sponsor is normally a supportive stakeholder given that they benefit from the results of the project. An example of a neutral stakeholder may be a government regulatory agency, as they do not have vested interest in the project's outcomes. For certain types of projects, activist groups who oppose the project are an example of an unsupportive stakeholder.

While not all stakeholders can or need to be supportive, moving stakeholders from unsupportive to supportive is usually positive for the project.

The following is the template for the **Stakeholder Analysis:**

Stakeholder Analysis Template

STAKEHOLDER ANALYSIS				
Project Name	[This section contains the project name that should appear consistently on all project documents. Organizations often have project naming conventions.]			
Name	**Project Role**	**Power**	**Interest**	**Level of Support**
[Name of the person or group.]	[Project role/title or the reason that they are a stakeholder.]	[High/ Low]	[High/ Low]	[Supportive/ Neutral/ Unsupportive]

Case Study Update: Creating the Stakeholder Analysis

After completing the Project Kickoff Meeting, Sophie starts to think about the planning work ahead. There are so many things to start working on. Her first priority is to create a list of all the stakeholders that she is aware of at this point in the project.

The company's CEO, Casey Serrador, is the first name on the list. By nature of her role, Casey has an extremely high level of power. Sophie knows from past experience that Casey's interest level is also high. Casey is a hands-on CEO who is fully engaged in the products of her company and is highly supportive of her employees.

Next, Sophie adds Arun Singh to the list. As the Project Sponsor, Arun has a high level of power. Arun will want this project to be successful and given the high visibility of this project, he will likely be very interested. She can count on a high level of support from him.

There will be three additional project teams working on the other DecoCam V4 Program projects—Development, Installation, and Technical Writing. Sophie has assessed that each of the Project Managers will possess a fairly high level of power, as their actions and decisions could positively or negatively affect her project. However, she knows that their primary interest will be in their project and therefore they will have a lower level of interest in hers. In terms of support, Sophie expects that they will be neutral.

In conversation with Arun, Sophie becomes aware of a potential issue. Jackson Woodhouse, Vice-President of Customer Support, is very upset that his project idea (upgraded camera software for a key customer) was bypassed in favour of the Photo Assistant option. Jackson is an important stakeholder and Sophie will need the cooperation of a number of people in his department. While Sophie feels his power and interest is high, she is worried about whether or not he will be supportive of her project. She will do her best to gain his support for the project, but she will assume that he will be unsupportive at this point in time.

At this point, there are no team members assigned to Sophie's project, but she knows that this will be changing soon. Part of the planning process is to identify and acquire the necessary team members to complete the project. For now, she adds *Project team* to her list, knowing that she will be able to fill in the names later. Her project team will have a lower level of power compared to other stakeholders. Their interest should be high and they should also be supportive. It will become an issue later if there are any uninterested or unsupportive team members assigned to the project.

And finally, there will be a number of other employees at Deco Productions who will be involved with or affected by the project. For example, they may provide services for or receive certain outputs of the project. In general, they will have a low level of power and interest, and their level of support will likely be neutral.

From past experience, Sophie knows that additional stakeholders will become apparent throughout the project and, as they do, she will add them to her list. For now, this is a good start.

The following is the Stakeholder Analysis for the project:

Stakeholder Analysis

STAKEHOLDER ANALYSIS				
Project Name	DCV4Launch–DecoCam V4 Product Launch			
Name	**Project Role**	**Power**	**Interest**	**Level of Support**
Casey Serrador	Founder and CEO	High	High	Supportive
Arun Singh	Project Sponsor	High	High	Supportive
Other V4 Project Managers	Project Managers of the other V4 projects	High	Low	Neutral
Jackson Woodhouse	Vice-President, Customer Support	High	High	Unsupportive
Project team	Project team	Low	High	Supportive
Deco Productions employees	Employees of Deco Productions with some level of contact with the project	Low	Low	Neutral

HOW CAN WE MANAGE THE STAKEHOLDERS?

The next step is to plan how to build or maintain effective relationships with each of the stakeholders that focus on their individual characteristics and needs. The Project Manager should proactively cultivate these relationships throughout the project.

While each stakeholder relationship is unique, some general approaches are as follows:

- *High power/high interest stakeholders*: while all stakeholders are significant to some degree, this type of stakeholder is a key player in the project. The Project Manager should pay close attention to this stakeholder and attempt to build as strong a relationship as possible.
- *High power/low interest stakeholders*: given their high degree of power, these stakeholders are also important. Their lower level of interest necessitates that the Project Manager's main priority is to understand the needs and requirements of this stakeholder and ensure they are met.
- *Low power/high interest stakeholders*: focus on providing this stakeholder with information that keeps them well-informed.
- *Low power/low interest stakeholders*: this stakeholder should be periodically monitored in order to detect any change in power or interest.

The template for the **Stakeholder Management Plan** is as follows:

Stakeholder Management Plan Template

STAKEHOLDER MANAGEMENT PLAN		
Project Name	[This section contains the project name that should appear consistently on all project documents. Organizations often have project naming conventions.]	
Name	**About the Stakeholder**	**Plan**
[Name of the person or group.]	[Background and characteristics of the stakeholder.]	[Details the approach to be taken to build an effective relationship with the stakeholder.]

Case Study Update: Creating the Stakeholder Management Plan

Sophie considers each of the stakeholders on her list. She asks herself the question: what can she do to build or enhance her relationship with them?

One of the approaches that has helped her when developing her stakeholder plan is to put herself in the shoes of each stakeholder. Once she does, she can more clearly evaluate their needs and decide how best to approach them.

The following is the Stakeholder Management Plan that was produced:

Stakeholder Management Plan

STAKEHOLDER MANAGEMENT PLAN		
Project Name	DCV4Launch–DecoCam V4 Product Launch	
Name	**About the Stakeholder**	**Plan**
Casey Serrador	As CEO of the company, Casey is an extremely important stakeholder. Casey is very outgoing and supportive, but she can be very demanding when it comes to the quality of her company's products and services. She does not tolerate people who are vague or evasive and she requires open and clear communication. She also promotes an open door policy that encourages employees to drop by her desk if they would like to talk to her.	• As part of this project, reports will not be provided directly to Casey, as Arun (Project Sponsor) will perform this task. • However, Casey is likely to make efforts to interact with the project team at various intervals. • Drop by her office periodically to demonstrate key aspects of the project (at least twice during the project). • Provide high-level overviews but be prepared to provide details if she requests more information. • Be open and direct with her regarding any requests for information. • Let the project team know that she may be dropping by for demos periodically.
Arun Singh	Arun is relatively new to the organization and seems concerned about creating a good first impression with this project. He is very supportive and friendly, but somewhat more reserved in nature compared to Casey's style of management. He has shown a great deal of interest in the financial aspects of the project and has expressed concern regarding the budget.	• Book informational meetings with Arun to provide him with updates and ensure that he is comfortable with the progress of the project. These can be held at increased or decreased intervals depending on his feedback. • Invite Arun to the bi-weekly team demonstration of completed deliverables. • Keep him updated regarding the budget information and alert him immediately if there is any indication that the budget will be exceeded.
Other V4 Project Managers	Many projects are interdependent, so it is important to foster positive relationships between the project teams.	• Schedule an initial meeting with each Project Manager to review their timeline and any dependencies between projects. • Respond to any requests for assistance and provide assistance when appropriate. • Send a summary of key dates to each Project Manager once the schedule is completed. Send updates to them if the key dates change during the project.

Continued

Jackson Woodhouse	Jackson has been with the organization for many years and is very loyal to the company. He has very strong convictions and is focused on providing support for Deco Productions' largest clients. In the past, he has been critical of the mobile device camera applications. He values direct discussion and likes to "tell it like it is."	• Early in the project, drop by Jackson's office to acknowledge and listen to his concerns about his preferred project option (upgraded camera software for a key customer). • Encourage his input and feedback. • During status update and reports, acknowledge the value of his department's support.
Project team	As the project team has not yet been assigned, this section cannot be completed. It is anticipated that experienced DecoCam employees will be assigned shortly.	• Keep the team well-informed by ensuring that all project documents are accessible. • Foster a positive team environment by periodically suggesting team lunches or gatherings at the end of the workday. • Check in with each team member regularly to see how their work is going and receive any feedback or concerns.
Deco Productions employees	The employees of the company are often interested in new products that are developed.	• No specific actions are planned at this time. • Answer any requests for information or updates when appropriate.

DISTRIBUTION OF STAKEHOLDER DOCUMENTS

While most of the project management documents described in this text are shared within the organization, the stakeholder documents contained in this chapter are generally not shared.

Since these stakeholder documents contain assessments of each stakeholder, they could be misinterpreted if read by a stakeholder, potentially harming the relationship. Therefore, care should be taken to keep these documents confidential.

CHAPTER SUMMARY

Key Concepts

1. Identify the stakeholders of the project.
2. Analyze their characteristics in order to determine their level of power, interest, and support.
3. Document this information in the Stakeholder Analysis.
4. Develop plans to interact with each stakeholder and document this information in the Stakeholder Management Plan.

Key Terminology

Interest: The stakeholder's level of concern or engagement that they have with a project.

Level of Support: The attitude the stakeholder displays toward the project, ranging from supportive to neutral to unsupportive.

Power: The stakeholder's ability to affect the project.

Stakeholder Analysis: A planning document listing the stakeholders of the project and including their perceived power, interest, and level of support.

Stakeholder Management Plan: A planning document containing the Project Manager's planned actions to manage each stakeholder relationship.

DISCUSSION QUESTIONS

1. Think of a project from your personal, work, or school activities. Identify the stakeholders for this endeavour.

2. Think of an example of a project stakeholder for each of the four combinations of power and interest:
   - High power, high interest
   - High power, low interest
   - Low power, high interest
   - Low power, low interest

3. What could cause a project stakeholder to change from being unsupportive to supportive?

4. What skills are most important in order to effectively manage project stakeholders?

5. Perform an online search researching the benefits of stakeholder management. Based on your findings, describe any additional benefits of stakeholder management not mentioned in the text.

4 Scope Planning

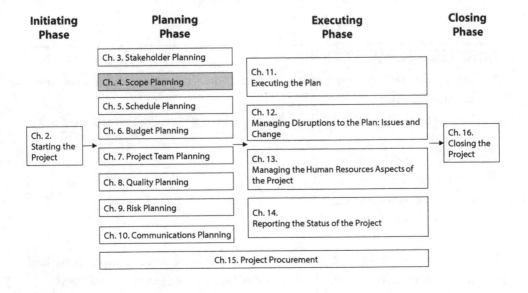

Initiating Phase	Planning Phase	Executing Phase	Closing Phase
	Ch. 3. Stakeholder Planning		
	Ch. 4. Scope Planning	Ch. 11. Executing the Plan	
	Ch. 5. Schedule Planning		
Ch. 2. Starting the Project	Ch. 6. Budget Planning	Ch. 12. Managing Disruptions to the Plan: Issues and Change	Ch. 16. Closing the Project
	Ch. 7. Project Team Planning	Ch. 13. Managing the Human Resources Aspects of the Project	
	Ch. 8. Quality Planning		
	Ch. 9. Risk Planning	Ch. 14. Reporting the Status of the Project	
	Ch. 10. Communications Planning		
	Ch. 15. Project Procurement		

INTRODUCTION TO SCOPE PLANNING

While the Project Charter defines the project's goals and objectives, it does not provide detailed information about what will be produced during the project. Therefore, additional planning should be performed in order to provide a clear definition of the requirements and details of the project's scope.

There are three main steps when planning the project scope:

Scope Planning

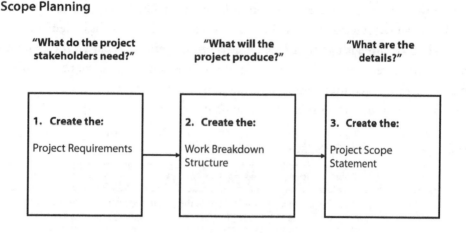

The first step is to determine the list of items needed for the project. These items are documented in the **Project Requirements**. The next step is to determine what the project will actually produce. The output of this step is the **Work Breakdown Structure**. The final step is to fully describe the features and characteristics of everything that will be produced. The output of this step is the **Project Scope Statement**.

WHAT DO THE PROJECT STAKEHOLDERS NEED?

The gathering of project requirements is an important first step as it allows the project team to understand the needs and wants of the Project Sponsor (or others within the organization as indicated by the Project Sponsor). The project requirements should support the goals and objectives that were documented in the Project Charter.

Project requirements may be gathered in a number of ways, and choosing an approach often depends on the number of individuals who are providing requirements. A common approach is to interview individuals within the organization. When there are a larger number of individuals providing requirements, approaches such as surveys, focus groups, and research may be more appropriate.

Discussions with the Project Sponsor will help identify the individuals who will provide requirements for the project. A challenge for the project team is to resolve any conflicting requirements from different individuals. The Project Sponsor can be consulted if needed to provide direction and resolve any disagreements.

When documenting requirements, it is often useful to separate the requirements into categories such as functional requirements, performance requirements, technical requirements, etc., depending on the project.

The following is the Project Requirements template:

Project Requirements Template

PROJECT REQUIREMENTS	
Project Name	[This section contains the project name that should appear consistently on all project documents. Organizations often have project naming conventions.]
Functional Requirements	
[This section should list the functional requirements for the project including any features or properties of the project's outcomes.]	
Technical/Performance Requirements	
[This section should list the technical requirements for the project (e.g., the required technology infrastructure) and any performance requirements (e.g., the minimum response time).]	

Case Study Update: Gathering the Project Requirements

Sophie sits at her desk and considers the recent Project Kickoff Meeting. While there were a few tough questions from the head of the software development division, it all went well. Picking up the Project Charter document, she scans the objectives for the project. She turns off the ringer on her phone to prevent any interruptions.

Sophie refreshes her memory by looking at the objectives. Based on the Business Case for the project, a full product launch is required including the support of the sales process, an update of DecoCam's website information, social media promotion, trade show materials, and the development of a promotional video.

While this is a good start, Sophie knows that these are high-level objectives. That is, the requirements for each of these objectives need additional detail in order for the scope of the project to be defined. The project has been approved with a $60,000 budget, so Sophie knows that the requirements need to fit within this budget amount.

In order to determine the project requirements, Sophie will need to bring a new member into her project team: a Business Analyst.

After negotiating with a couple of senior managers within the company, Sophie secures Jason Brown for a period of time. Jason was one of the company's first employees and has worked in both the administrative and marketing areas of the company. He has recently moved into a Business Analyst position and his in-depth knowledge of the company has been very useful during recent projects.

Jason meets with a number of individuals within the Product Development and Marketing departments in order to understand their needs. He also reviews the approaches that were taken when similar products were launched, while also checking to see the impact the approaches had on the subsequent sales activity. Jason documents this information in the Project Requirements document.

What follows is the resulting Project Requirements document:

Project Requirements

PROJECT REQUIREMENTS	
Project Name	DCV4Launch–DecoCam V4 Product Launch

Functional Requirements

1. All DecoCam product information listed on the company website and printed materials should be updated to include Version 4 and the key characteristics of this version.
2. Promotional material should be distributed through sponsored advertisements on selected websites and through Deco Productions' social media presence.
3. A press release for this version should be created.
4. The technology blogging community should be engaged so that they cover the new release.
5. The promotional video should be professional and engaging, and should demonstrate the key features of the new version.
6. Materials should be produced for upcoming trade shows and include DecoCam signs, booth giveaways branded with the DecoCam logo, and a multimedia display that will draw trade show attendees to the booth.
7. The trade show materials should be delivered and set up at each trade show.

Technical/Performance Requirements

1. All promotional files and videos should be compatible with all major browsers and operating systems.
2. All files should be created in PDF format.
3. All promotional files to be accessed by customers should be under 10 MB to ensure minimal download times.

WHAT WILL THE PROJECT PRODUCE?

Once the requirements are known, the **scope** of the project may be defined. The scope is the product, service, or result created during the project. The first step in defining the scope is to create a Work Breakdown Structure (WBS) for the project.

Case Study Update: Creating the Work Breakdown Structure

Now that the project requirements have been defined, the planning team (Sophie and Jason) can begin to define the work that needs to be completed. Rather than viewing this product launch as one large effort, Sophie breaks the project into smaller chunks of work to make it easier to define and manage.

Building on the work already completed (i.e., the Business Case, Project Charter, and Project Requirements documents) and their past experience on other projects, Sophie and Jason decide that they will need to support the trade shows through the creation of signage, a demo, a product sheet, and possibly some branded items to give away at the booths. In the area of media and industry relations, a press release will be created and an outreach to the blogger community will be performed. There are also a number of promotional items that will need to be produced, including website updates, social media, and the new video.

Sophie and Jason identify that one of the requirements is to deliver and display the new materials at the trade shows. After some consideration and discussion with the Project Sponsor and other stakeholders, they decide that the project team will not perform this requirement, but instead the Marketing department trade show team will be given the necessary materials before the events.

From this discussion, Sophie decides that there are three main categories of work for the project and writes the following on a notepad:

1. Trade Show Support
2. Communications
3. Promotional Video

She then breaks down each category as follows:

1. Trade Show Support
    1.1 Trade Show Signage
    1.2 Booth Giveaways
    1.3 Multimedia Demo

2.   Communications
    2.1 Press Release
    2.2 Media Outreach
    2.3 Social Media
    2.4 Website Updates
3.   Promotional Video

Looking at this list, Sophie feels a sense of relief. The product launch is large and complex and she wasn't quite sure where to start. But by breaking the project down into smaller chunks of work, she now sees the project as a series of eight smaller, simpler subprojects.

When Sophie breaks the project down into categories (Trade Show Support, Communications, Promotional Video), she is defining the **deliverables** that will be produced. A deliverable is something that is produced during the project. Deliverables may be something that the customer(s) of the project receives (e.g., the promotional video) or they may be something internal to the project (e.g., the script required in order to produce the promotional video).

When defining the WBS, the idea is to continue to break down each deliverable until the work involved is understood and may be assigned to a person or team for completion. A WBS contains all of the deliverables to be produced during the project. In order for something to be produced during the project, it needs to be included in the WBS—if it isn't in the WBS, it won't be done.

A WBS consists of deliverables at various levels. For the case study, there are three high-level deliverables: Trade Show Support, Communications, and the Promotional Video. High-level deliverables may be broken down into smaller deliverables. A deliverable at the lowest level of a WBS (i.e., a deliverable that is not broken down further) is also referred to as a **work package**.

There are various approaches that may be used to create a WBS:

- A top-down approach to identify the high-level deliverables and then progressively break them down into their work packages. This is the approach used in the case study.
- A bottom-up approach to first identify work packages and then group them together to create the structure of the WBS. This can be a useful approach when the high-level deliverables are not obvious to the project team.

- An approach using a similar project's WBS as a starting point and then making changes as appropriate.
- An approach using a standard WBS as defined by an organization.

When creating a WBS, a combination of any of the above approaches may be used. The goal is to develop an effective WBS that contains everything that needs to be produced during the project.

A common question when creating a WBS is determining when to stop breaking deliverables down into smaller deliverables. A good approach to use is that a deliverable does not need to be broken down further if the person or team responsible for its creation understands the work involved.

While a WBS should contain all of the deliverables to be produced, there is information that should not be included:

- Scheduling information: a WBS does not contain dates or indicate the order that the work will be performed. Deliverables and work packages should be considered to be listed at random.
- Cost information: a WBS does not contain any cost information.
- Detailed specifications: a WBS does not contain a description of the deliverables.

Technically, a WBS would also include all project management deliverables produced during the project, including work packages such as the Project Charter, Project Requirements, and Project Scope Statement. However, in practice, many Project Managers do not include their own activities within the WBS as they are understood to be included within the scope of the project.

WHAT ARE THE DETAILS?

When defining the scope of the project, it is important to determine the characteristics of the work packages in the WBS. Determining this information often involves a series of meetings, conversations, emails, and other communications over a period of time ranging from days to months. In order to ensure that everyone involved in the project has access to the same information, the work package characteristics should be summarized and documented in the Project Scope Statement.

The Project Scope Statement also explicitly defines what is not included in the project. For example, in the case study, the decision was made that the project team would not be involved in the set up of new materials at trade shows. To help ensure that everyone is aware of this decision, the Project Scope Statement should state that this work is not to be performed.

The advantage of creating this document is that it becomes the document of record for the project and may be used to verify the scope with the Project Sponsor and other stakeholders. It is a key communication tool to ensure that there is a common understanding of the project scope. The Project Sponsor should provide specific approval of the Project Scope Statement.

The following is the Project Scope Statement template:

Project Scope Statement Template

PROJECT SCOPE STATEMENT	
Project Name	[This section contains the project name that should appear consistently on all project documents. Organizations often have project naming conventions.]
Project Deliverables	
[High-level deliverable from the WBS is listed here.]	[Work package listed here.] [Describe this work package in as much detail as possible.] [Work package listed here.] [Describe this work package in as much detail as possible.]
[High-level deliverable from the WBS is listed here.]	[Work package listed here.] [Describe this work package in as much detail as possible.] [Work package listed here.] [Describe this work package in as much detail as possible.]
Project Exclusions	
[Indicate anything that will not be included in the scope of the project.]	

Case Study Update: Creating the Project Scope Statement

As Sophie reflects on her planning up to this point, she is feeling more confident. She has a good handle on the project requirements and she understands the work that needs to be completed now that she has created a Work Breakdown Structure.

Continued

Yet the more she thinks about the next steps, the more she feels uneasy. Sophie's natural tendency is to want to get going on the project rather than writing down the details. However, during some of her recent projects, this approach has caused problems later on. One or more of the following would usually take place:

- Even though details were discussed with the Project Sponsor and other stakeholders, memories of the discussion and decisions would fade over time. There were often disagreements about what was or was not to be included in the project.
- Team members working on the project were often confused about what they were meant to produce.
- Small details were missed, causing a number of last minute emergencies.

After her last project when each of the above problems occurred, Sophie resolved that she would fully document the scope for her future projects.

The following is the Project Scope Statement for the case study project:

Project Scope Statement

PROJECT SCOPE STATEMENT	
Project Name	DCV4Launch–DecoCam V4 Product Launch
Project Deliverables	
Trade Show Support	Trade Show Signage • The signs will be retractable banner stands. • Initial creation of five stands. • Integrate with company's existing trade show set up and branding. • Provide a visual display of the product's features. • Display information with links to more product information. • Update the trade show supplies procedures and data files to allow for the order of additional banners.
	Booth Giveaways • Consists of a flyer that resembles a postcard. • Initial creation of 2,000 postcards. • The picture side of the postcard will contain a holographic scene of an art deco building with a sign displaying the DecoCam name and logo. • The address side of the postcard will contain the necessary product and contact information. • Update the trade show supplies procedures and data files to allow for the order of additional postcards.

	Multimedia Demo • Consists of a mural showing an urban scene for visual interest. • A mobile phone will be mounted on a tripod and will run a slideshow simulating the user experience of using the DecoCam Photo Assistant feature. • Initial creation of two murals and the set up of two tripods with phones. • Update the trade show supplies procedures and data files to allow for the order of additional demo kits.
Communications	Press Release • Create a one-page news story following The Canadian Press style. • Distribute electronically to media on the same date that DecoCam V4 is available for download to the public.
	Media Outreach • Includes email and phone calls to encourage publicity from major online influencers (e.g., industry magazines, top technology bloggers).
	Social Media • Develop a social media strategy and calendar for the three months following the launch of the product. • Develop the content for the planned social media posts.
	Website Updates • Update the DecoCam product page to include the features of the new version. • Create an online slideshow that demonstrates the key features of the new version.
Promotions	Promotional Video • Develop a professional video that demonstrates how to use the new product. • To increase the likelihood that viewers will share the video through social media channels, the video should contain a humorous situation. • The message of the video will be the usefulness of the DecoCam Photo Assistant feature and how it will help average people take photos like a professional photographer. • The video should be no more than two minutes in length.

Project Exclusions

Distribution of social media posts. This will be performed by the marketing department.

Distribution of the DecoCam software. This will be performed by the DecoCam V4 Installation Project.

Trade show staffing and management. Documentation and supplies for the trade shows will be created and will be available for order by the marketing department.

Technical support for the website content, videos, or other materials. This will be provided by the marketing department.

OTHER SUPPORTING DOCUMENTS

While the Project Scope Statement contains a description of what is (and is not) contained in the scope of the project, there are often additional details that do not fit easily into the structure of the Project Scope Statement. The Project Scope Statement may refer to other supporting documents, such as:

- mural design and layout information;
- promotional video storyboard and script information;
- online slideshow design; or
- other documents that support the description of the project scope.

In summary, the scope of the project consists of the Project Requirements, the WBS, the Project Scope Statement, and all of the supporting documents that describe the content of the project.

CHAPTER SUMMARY

Key Concepts

1. Gather the project requirements from the project stakeholders.
2. Create a Work Breakdown Structure (WBS) that defines the deliverables to be created during the project.
3. Create a Project Scope Statement that describes the deliverables contained in the WBS.
4. Supporting documents that describe the scope of the project may be appended to the Project Scope Statement in order to more fully describe the project scope.

Key Terminology

Deliverable: Something that is produced during the project. The collection of all deliverables comprises the scope of the project.

Project Requirements: A planning document that describes the items and capabilities needed for project output.

Project Scope Statement: A planning document that fully describes the deliverables contained in the WBS.

Scope: The product, service, or result created during the project.

Work Breakdown Structure: A hierarchical document listing the project deliverables to be produced during the project.

Work Package: A deliverable that is at the lowest level of the WBS and is not further divided into sub-deliverables.

DISCUSSION QUESTIONS

1. Think of a new product that you may be planning to purchase over the next year (e.g., phone, vacation). Make a list of the requirements for this purchase. Group your requirements into categories, such as functional, technical, and performance requirements.

2. What is the benefit of creating a Work Breakdown Structure? Why is it more effective to create a WBS and a Project Scope Statement, rather than just a Project Scope Statement?

3. How much detail should be documented in the Project Scope Statement? When should you stop defining additional details?

4. Perform an online search to research how a lack of scope planning can lead to project failures. Summarize your findings.

5   Schedule Planning

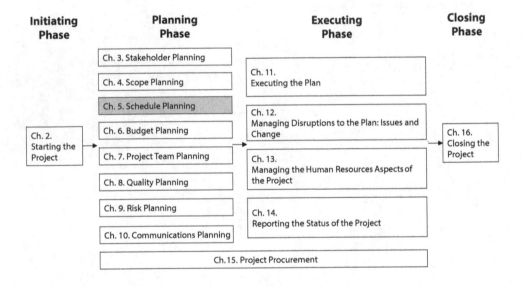

Initiating Phase	Planning Phase	Executing Phase	Closing Phase
	Ch. 3. Stakeholder Planning	Ch. 11. Executing the Plan	
	Ch. 4. Scope Planning		
	Ch. 5. Schedule Planning	Ch. 12. Managing Disruptions to the Plan: Issues and Change	
Ch. 2. Starting the Project	Ch. 6. Budget Planning		Ch. 16. Closing the Project
	Ch. 7. Project Team Planning	Ch. 13. Managing the Human Resources Aspects of the Project	
	Ch. 8. Quality Planning		
	Ch. 9. Risk Planning	Ch. 14. Reporting the Status of the Project	
	Ch. 10. Communications Planning		
	Ch. 15. Project Procurement		

INTRODUCTION TO SCHEDULE PLANNING

Once the project scope is defined, the next step is to create a schedule. The development of a schedule is beneficial for the following reasons:

- It allows the project team to make commitments to its stakeholders about the final delivery date as well as interim deliverables.
- Everyone involved in the project is able to see their efforts within the context of the whole project and understand the connections and interdependencies that may exist.
- It provides an established project timeline that may be used to track the progress of the project. This established timeline is known as a **baseline**.

There are two main steps when planning the project timeline:

Schedule Planning

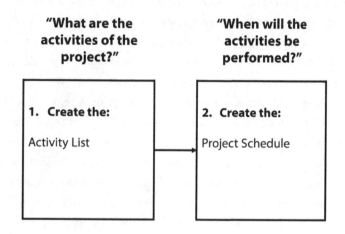

The first step is to create a list of the project activities required to complete the project. The next step is to arrange the activities in logical order.

WHAT ARE THE ACTIVITIES OF THE PROJECT?

For each deliverable of the project, the activities needed to create the deliverable are defined. Depending on the project, a larger number of detailed activities or a smaller number of general activities may be needed. To help determine the number of activities, the following criteria can be used:

- Each activity should be clear to those who will perform the activity. If it is unclear, additional activities are required.
- The **duration** of each activity (i.e., the total amount of time available for the activity) should be moderate. Extremely long activity durations (e.g., 30 days) may be challenging to manage, especially if the work is complex. Extremely short activity durations (e.g., 10 minutes) will result in a large number of activities that in turn increase the size and complexity of the resulting schedule.
- Each activity should have an identifiable person or group who will be responsible for its completion.

Case Study Update: Creating the Activity List

It's Monday morning and Sophie arrives early to the office, coffee in hand, ready to continue with the planning of the project. To refresh her memory, she reads through the draft WBS and Project Scope Statement that she and Jason created last week.

Sophie takes a simple approach to get started. First, she considers the list of work packages that were previously documented: the Trade Show Signage, Booth Giveaways, Multimedia Demo, Press Release, Media Outreach, Social Media, Website Updates, and Promotional Video. Next, she writes each work package on a separate blank piece of paper. She titles another document *Project Management* to reflect on the work necessary to manage this project. Then, she brainstorms about each work package and begins to list their required activities. This helps her compartmentalize the work required to get each work package and the project management done. It's a big job—when she's finished, there will be nine pieces of paper filled with activities, but Sophie knows she'll produce a better estimate and execute a better project as a result of her planning.

After about 30 minutes, Sophie completes the **Activity List** for the project:

Activity List

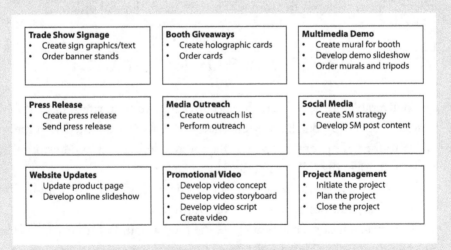

Trade Show Signage	**Booth Giveaways**	**Multimedia Demo**
• Create sign graphics/text • Order banner stands	• Create holographic cards • Order cards	• Create mural for booth • Develop demo slideshow • Order murals and tripods
Press Release	**Media Outreach**	**Social Media**
• Create press release • Send press release	• Create outreach list • Perform outreach	• Create SM strategy • Develop SM post content
Website Updates	**Promotional Video**	**Project Management**
• Update product page • Develop online slideshow	• Develop video concept • Develop video storyboard • Develop video script • Create video	• Initiate the project • Plan the project • Close the project

WHEN WILL THE ACTIVITIES BE PERFORMED?

Now that a list of activities has been determined, the next step is to create the schedule for the project. This involves considering the timing of the activities.

This timing of activities is based on:

- the required sequence of activities based on the work involved, also known as determining the **dependencies** between activities;
- the completion of activities by a certain date.

Case Study Update: Determining When the Activities Will Be Performed

Sophie examines the nine pieces of paper full of project activities. While she has captured the work to be done, she knows she needs to put the activities in some kind of order or sequence. The Trade Show Signage activities, for example, don't all happen at the same time. So, with a pad of sticky notes in hand, Sophie takes the Trade Show Signage work package and copies the two activities—*create sign graphics/text* and *order banner stands*—onto separate sticky notes. She does the same for the remaining pages of activities and arranges them onto her office whiteboard as follows:

Project Activities

Create sign graphics/text	Order banner stands	Create holographic cards
Order cards	Create mural for booth	Develop demo slideshow
Order murals and tripods	Create press release	Send press release
Create outreach list	Perform outreach	Create SM strategy
Create SM post content	Update product page	Develop online slideshow
Develop video concept	Develop video storyboard	Develop video script
Create video	Initiate the project	Plan the project
Close the project		

Next, Sophie begins to rearrange the sticky notes to put them in the order that they should be performed. Her experience with previous product launches helps her determine the correct order.

For example, Sophie determines that the following activities are sequential (i.e., performed in a particular order) so she arranges them as follows and draws a line between them.

Continued

Sequential Activities

| Create sign graphics/text |—| Order banner stands |

Sophie finds that there are some activities that are not related to each other and may be performed at the same time if necessary. For example, the *create SM strategy* and *develop video concept* activities in the Social Media work package do not need to be performed in any particular order. For these activities, a line is not drawn between them on the whiteboard. They appear as follows:

Unrelated Activities

| Create SM strategy |

| Develop video concept |

Another factor that Sophie needs to consider is the number of people who will be assigned to the project and their project roles. Based on the work required for this project, she writes the following human resources requirements on her notepad:

- Graphic Designer: needed to complete the Trade Show Signage, Booth Giveaways, and Multimedia Demo work packages
- Communications Specialist: needed to complete the Press Release, Media Outreach, Social Media, and Website Updates work packages
- Marketing Specialist: needed to complete the Promotional Video work package
- Videographer: needed to complete the Promotional Video work package

In addition, a Business Analyst (Jason Brown) was assigned to help plan the project scope. Sophie's expertise as Project Manager will also be needed throughout the project.

As Sophie arranges the papers on the whiteboard, the timeline of the project is becoming clear.

Creating the Network Diagram

A useful tool for displaying the sequence of activities is a **network diagram,** which displays the project's activities as follows:

- Each activity is represented by a rectangle.
- The network diagram is read from left to right on the page.
- The lines indicate a dependency between the activities.

Based on the order of activities, the following is the network diagram created for the case study project.

Network Diagram

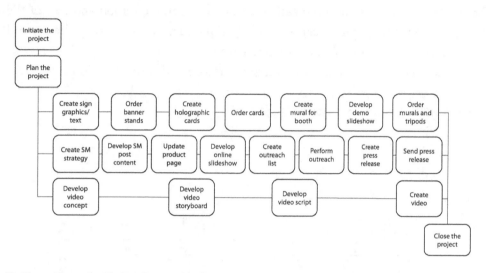

Estimating Activity Duration

An important characteristic of each activity is the estimated duration. Developing accurate duration estimates can be challenging for a number of reasons:

- Given the unique nature of projects, the activity may not have been performed before, making it difficult to determine its likely duration.
- Unforeseen problems can cause the activity to take longer than estimated.
- The expertise of the person(s) working on the activity affects the duration. Often, their identity is not known when the estimate is created.

There are a number of techniques that are helpful when creating duration estimates, including the following:

- Using the experience of past projects as a guideline for the current estimate. This may be based on the experience of the person making the estimation or through consultation with others.
- Analyzing the actual work required for the activity in order to develop the estimate.

When creating activity duration estimates, the more detailed the scope of the project, the more accurate the estimates tend to be.

Given the difficulty and potential for inaccuracy when estimating duration, it is usually advisable to allow extra time in the activity for unforeseen work or issues. This is known as adding contingency to the duration. This contingency may be placed in each activity duration estimate or as a total amount at the end of the project. However, the use of contingency time may not be viewed positively by all stakeholders. Some may view it as an attempt by the project team to pad the estimates and needlessly increase the overall duration and cost of the project. Effective communication is required in order to demonstrate the use and benefit of allotting or using contingency time.

The following is the network diagram updated with the duration estimates:

Network Diagram with Duration Displayed

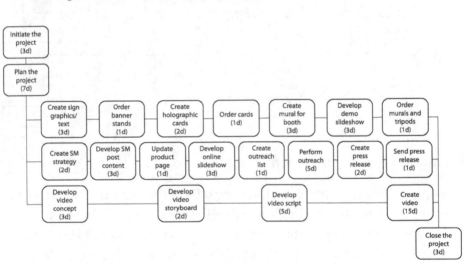

The main benefit of creating a network diagram is that it clearly displays the order of the activities and in particular the dependencies between the activities.

However, network diagrams are not effective at displaying the dates that activities are planned for and are difficult to maintain throughout the project. Because of these limitations, they are often useful for initial planning purposes but are not subsequently maintained throughout the project.

Project Schedules

As noted above, while network diagrams may be useful for planning purposes, they are not generally maintained throughout the project. Instead, there are a number of other schedule formats that may be used, each with their own advantages and disadvantages. Choosing what format to use should be based on the project's characteristics, including its size, complexity, and the likelihood that alterations or changes may occur.

The following are the three different schedule formats that may be used:
- Milestone-based schedule
- Activity-based schedule
- Dependency-based schedule

The Milestone-Based Schedule

Milestones are important events that occur during a project. They are not regular activities that are measured by the duration and work involved, but are instead an indicator that something significant has been completed during the project.

Milestones were first defined during the creation of the Project Charter. They are often further defined during planning.

The **milestone-based schedule** for the case study project is as follows:

Milestone-Based Schedule

MILESTONE	DATE
Project approved	March 25, 2020
Trade show materials complete	April 23, 2020
Communications complete	April 29, 2020
Promotional video complete	May 8, 2020
Project complete	May 13, 2020

Milestone-based schedules are simple to use and understand, can be easily accessed by team members and stakeholders, and will likely require minimal updates during the project.

However, since activities are not contained in the schedule, they will need to be managed outside of the schedule. This may make it more difficult to plan for project costs and resources.

Milestone-based schedules are often appropriate for small and/or simple projects.

The Activity-Based Schedule

The **activity-based schedule** contains the project's activities and includes information such as the duration, start date, and end date of each activity. The activity-based schedule for the case study project is as follows:

Activity-Based Schedule

ACTIVITY	DURATION	START DATE	END DATE
Initiating			
Initiate the project	3 days	March 23, 2020	March 25, 2020
Project approved	0 days	March 25, 2020	March 25, 2020
Planning			
Plan the project	7 days	March 26, 2020	April 3, 2020
Executing			
Trade Show Signage			
Create sign graphics/text	3 days	April 6, 2020	April 8, 2020
Order banner stands	1 day	April 9, 2020	April 9, 2020
Booth Giveaways			
Create holographic cards	2 days	April 10, 2020	April 13, 2020
Order cards	1 day	April 14, 2020	April 14, 2020
Multimedia Demo			
Create mural for booth	3 days	April 15, 2020	April 17, 2020
Develop demo slideshow	3 days	April 20, 2020	April 22, 2020
Order murals and tripods	1 day	April 23, 2020	April 23, 2020
Trade show materials complete	0 days	April 23, 2020	April 23, 2020
Social Media			
Create SM strategy	2 days	April 6, 2020	April 7, 2020
Develop SM post content	3 days	April 8, 2020	April 10, 2020
Website Updates			
Update product page	1 day	April 13, 2020	April 13, 2020
Develop online slideshow	3 days	April 14, 2020	April 16, 2020
Media Outreach			
Create outreach list	1 day	April 17, 2020	April 17, 2020
Perform outreach	5 days	April 20, 2020	April 24, 2020
Press Release			
Create press release	2 days	April 27, 2020	April 28, 2020
Send press release	1 day	April 29, 2020	April 29, 2020
Communications complete	0 days	April 29, 2020	April 29, 2020
Promotional Video			
Develop video concept	3 days	April 6, 2020	April 8, 2020
Develop video storyboard	2 days	April 9, 2020	April 10, 2020

Develop video script	5 days	April 13, 2020	Apr 17, 2020
Create video	15 days	April 20, 2020	May 8, 2020
Promotional video complete	0 days	May 8, 2020	May 8, 2020
Closing			
Close the project	3 days	May 11, 2020	May 13, 2020
Project complete	0 days	May 13, 2020	May 13, 2020

For certain types of projects that have fixed end dates, such as events, a **work-back schedule** may be used. A work-back schedule is a specific type of activity-based schedule in which the timing of each activity is determined by working backward from the project's end date. For example, during the case study, the project must be complete (except for the project closing) by May 8th. Working backward from this date, it is determined that:

- the video script should be created three weeks before this date (April 17th);
- the video storyboard should be created four weeks before this date (April 10th).

Using this work-back method, the remainder of the activities are planned relative to the project's end date.

Activity-based schedules may also be implemented as a series of lists using a workflow approach, such as a Kanban schedule. Kanban is a scheduling system originally developed at Toyota to improve its manufacturing process.

Using this method, a board representing the project is divided into multiple lists. Each list contains activities at different stages of the project. For example, the board may be set up to contain three lists: To-Do, Doing, and Done. At the start of the project, all activities are contained in the To-Do list. The project team will then select which tasks to work on first and move them to the Doing list. As activities are completed, they are moved to the Done list. At any point in the project, the content of the board visually demonstrates the status of the project.

Using a workflow approach, the case study project would appear as follows during the third week of the project:

Activity-Based Schedule Using a Workflow Approach

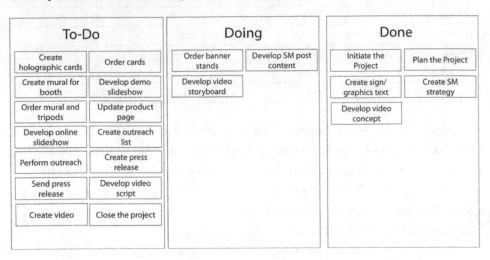

Activity-based schedules are simple to use, straightforward to update, and may be easily accessed by team members and stakeholders during the project.

However, this type of schedule does not demonstrate the dependencies that may be present between activities. Changes to the timing of activities during the project could cause problems if these dependencies are not considered.

Activity-based schedules are often appropriate for small to medium-sized projects.

The Dependency-Based Schedule

Similar to the activity-based schedule, the **dependency-based schedule** contains all project activities along with their durations, start dates, and end dates. Additionally, this type of schedule displays any dependencies that may be present between activities.

This type of schedule is usually created using project management software and displayed in the **Gantt Chart** format. The Gantt Chart is named after Henry Gantt, an engineer and management consultant who developed the project management tool during the 1910s.

A Gantt Chart is divided into two sections. On the left side is a spreadsheet with each row representing an activity of the project. On the right side is a timeline made up of horizontal bars that represent the duration and timing of each activity. Dependencies are represented by an arrow between activities. Milestones are represented by a diamond shape.

The following is the dependency-based schedule for the case study project using the Gantt Chart format:

Dependency-Based Schedule (Gantt Chart)

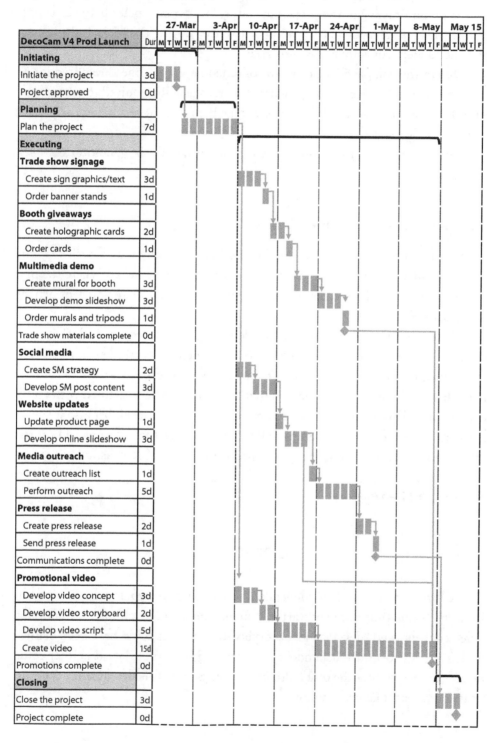

The main advantage of the dependency-based schedule is that it clearly demonstrates the timeline of the project including the dependencies between activities. If changes are made to the timing of activities during the project, the impact on other dependent activities is displayed.

Due to the complexity of this type of schedule, more time is required for its maintenance and project management software is usually required to view or update the schedule. This results in the schedule being less accessible to the project team and other stakeholders.

Dependency-based schedules may be appropriate for large and/or complex projects.

More About Activity Dependencies

Up to this point, all the dependencies described are known as Finish-to-Start (FS) dependencies. This is the most common type of dependency where the first activity must finish before the second activity may start. The majority of dependencies are FS.

There are other, less common dependency types that may occur during projects. A Start-to-Start (SS) dependency occurs when two activities must start at the same time but may finish at different times. For example, the "create outreach list" and "perform outreach" activities could have been defined with an SS dependency. This would be appropriate if creating the outreach list also involved performing outreach (e.g., testing some of the names that were placed on the outreach list). This dependency type appears on a Gantt Chart as follows:

Start-to-Start Dependency

| Create outreach list | 1d |
| Perform outreach | 5d |

A Finish-to-Finish (FF) dependency occurs when two activities must finish at the same time but may start at different times. For example, the "develop video concept" and "develop video storyboard" activities could have been defined with a Finish-to-Finish dependency. This would be appropriate if neither could be completed without the other also being completed. This dependency type appears on a Gantt Chart as follows:

Finish-to-Finish Dependency

A Start-to-Finish (SF) dependency occurs in the following situation: only when an activity starts, another activity may then finish. This dependency type is extremely rare and will not be demonstrated in this text.

Dependency Leads and Lags

Up to this point, when Activity A finishes, Activity B may start. While this is a simple way to think of activities, in real life, things are often more complex. For example, as Activity A is winding down, Activity B may be ramping up, and they may overlap to some degree. In scheduling terminology, this is known as a **lead**. The following demonstrates a two-day lead between the "develop video script" and "create video" activities:

Dependency with a Two-Day Lead

Develop video script	5d
Create video	15d

There may be times when a gap between activities is required. This is known as a **lag**. Lags may be included in the schedule for a number of reasons, including a required break due to the nature of the work or the unavailability of the required resources. For example, in order to send the press release at a more appropriate time, a two-day lag could be introduced between the activities "create press release" and "send press release."

Dependency with a One-Day Lag

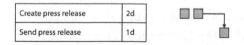

CRITICAL PATH ANALYSIS—AN OVERVIEW

For projects that use activity dependency-based schedules, it is possible to calculate the **critical path** of the project. The critical path is the longest sequence of activities in the project schedule. This sequence of activities represents the earliest planned completion time for the project.

Critical Path Analysis—A Simple Example

In order to demonstrate the critical path concept, consider the following network diagram:

Critical Path Example

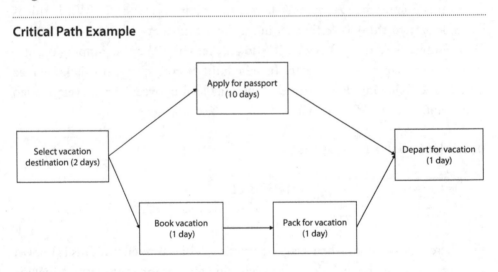

For this project, there are two paths through the network:

- Select vacation destination → apply for passport → depart for vacation (13 days)
- Select vacation destination → book vacation → pack for vacation → depart for vacation (5 days)

The first path (13 days) is the critical path since it is the longest sequence of dependent tasks and therefore represents the earliest time that this project may be completed. In other words, it would take 13 days for you to be sitting in an airport, with your tickets, suitcases, and passport in hand.

It also indicates the relative importance of each activity from a time perspective. For example, on the third day, there are two activities that may be started: "apply for passport" and "book the vacation." The process of booking the vacation may be more interesting to you than the task of applying for a passport. However, because applying for the passport is on the critical path, any delay to this activity would delay the entire project. Knowledge of the critical path can help guide you to ensure the passport activity is given the higher priority.

Another concept related to the critical path is **total float**. Total float is the amount of time an activity may be delayed before it delays the project end date. A related concept is known as **free float**. Free float is the amount of time an activity may be delayed before it delays a subsequent task or the project end date. Throughout the remainder of this text, total float will be discussed and calculated.

By definition, all activities on the critical path have zero total float in that a delay in any activity on the critical path will delay the end of the project. The two activities that are not on the critical path—"book vacation" and "pack for vacation"—share a total of eight days of float. This can be deduced by calculating that during the ten days required for the "apply for passport" activity, two days are required to complete the "book vacation" and "pack for vacation" activities. This leaves eight remaining days of total float. Therefore, the two activities may be delayed up to eight days without impacting the project's completion date.

Critical Path Analysis—The Case Study Project

The critical path can now be determined for the case study project. Looking at the network diagram there are three paths through the network as follows:

- Path 1 (27 days): The path starting with "initiate the project" and "plan the project," through to the activities ranging from "create sign graphics/text" to "order murals and tripods," and ending with "close the project."
- Path 2 (31 days): The path starting with "initiate the project" and "plan the project," through to the activities ranging from "create SM strategy" to "send press release," and ending with "close the project."
- Path 3 (38 days): The path starting with "initiate the project" and "plan the project," through to the activities ranging from "develop video concept" to "create video," and ending with "close the project."

As shown below, Path 3 is the longest and is therefore the critical path:

Network Diagram with Critical Path Displayed

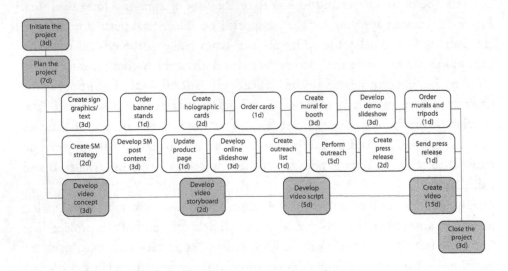

The time span of the critical path (38 days) also defines the total planned project duration. All tasks on the critical path (highlighted on the network diagram above) contain zero float. This means that if any of the critical path tasks are delayed, all subsequent activities on the critical path will also be delayed, resulting in a delay of the project.

To determine the total float in the non-critical path activities, refer to the following network diagram. The critical path activities ranging from "develop video concept" to "create video" in Path 3 have a total duration of 25 days. Conversely, the non-critical activities ranging from "create sign graphics/text" to "order murals and tripods" in Path 1 have a total duration of 14 days. The amount of total float contained in these activities is 11 days (25 days – 14 days). This means that these activities in Path 1 may be delayed by up to 11 days before delaying the completion of the project.

Using the same calculation, the activities ranging from "create SM strategy" to "send press release" in Path 2 have a total duration of 18 days, resulting in 7 days of total float (25 days – 18 days). The activities in Path 2 may be delayed up to 7 days before delaying the completion of the project.

Network Diagram with Total Float Displayed

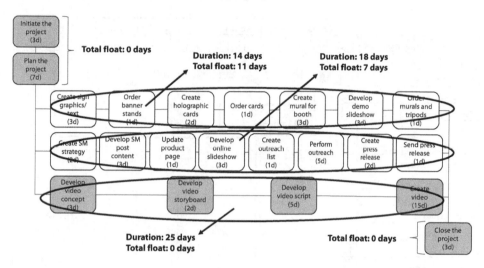

The Gantt Chart displaying the critical path is shown on page 66. While determining the critical path and total float is relatively straightforward for simple schedules, it is much more difficult for larger or complex projects. For these types of projects, project management software may be used to automate the critical path calculations.

CRITICAL PATH ANALYSIS—THE CALCULATIONS

This section demonstrates the calculations that are required to determine the critical path and the amount of total float for a schedule. They are included here to provide a deeper understanding of the critical path and total scope, and not to suggest that they have to be manually calculated during a project.

Calculating the critical path involves looking at the schedule in two distinct ways:

1. Determining the earliest date that each activity may occur by performing a **forward pass** of the schedule. This will determine the **Early Start (ES)** and **Early Finish (EF)** times for each activity.
2. Determining the latest date that each activity may occur by performing a **backward pass** of the schedule. This will determine the **Late Start (LS)** and **Late Finish (LF)** times for each activity.

Dependency-Based Schedule (Gantt Chart) with Critical Path

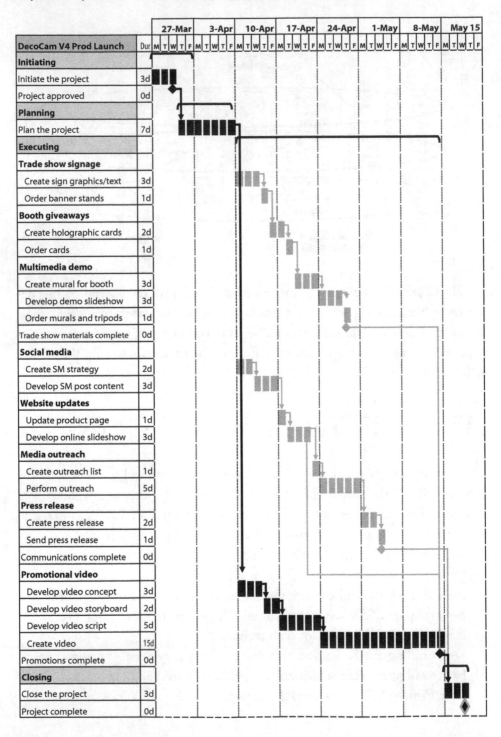

DecoCam V4 Prod Launch	Dur	27-Mar	3-Apr	10-Apr	17-Apr	24-Apr	1-May	8-May	May 15
Initiating									
Initiate the project	3d								
Project approved	0d								
Planning									
Plan the project	7d								
Executing									
Trade show signage									
Create sign graphics/text	3d								
Order banner stands	1d								
Booth giveaways									
Create holographic cards	2d								
Order cards	1d								
Multimedia demo									
Create mural for booth	3d								
Develop demo slideshow	3d								
Order murals and tripods	1d								
Trade show materials complete	0d								
Social media									
Create SM strategy	2d								
Develop SM post content	3d								
Website updates									
Update product page	1d								
Develop online slideshow	3d								
Media outreach									
Create outreach list	1d								
Perform outreach	5d								
Press release									
Create press release	2d								
Send press release	1d								
Communications complete	0d								
Promotional video									
Develop video concept	3d								
Develop video storyboard	2d								
Develop video script	5d								
Create video	15d								
Promotions complete	0d								
Closing									
Close the project	3d								
Project complete	0d								

Critical Path Calculations—A Simple Example

To demonstrate the forward pass, the vacation project introduced earlier in this chapter will be used.

The Forward Pass

In this example, each activity will be assigned a Task ID as follows:

Task IDs for the Vacation Project

Task ID	Activity
A	Select vacation destination
B	Apply for passport
C	Book vacation
D	Pack for vacation
E	Depart for vacation

On the network diagram, each activity will display the Task ID and duration as follows:

Displaying the Task ID and Duration in the Network Diagram

The resulting network diagram is as follows:

Vacation Project with Task IDs

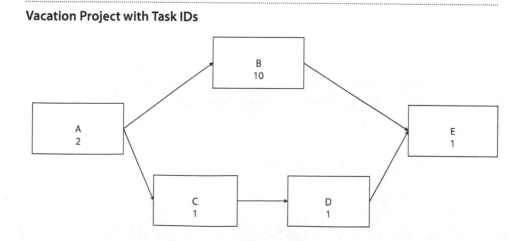

The method to calculate the early start (ES) and early finish (EF) of each activity is as follows.

For activities that have no predecessors (i.e., the first activities in the schedule):

1. Set ES = 1
2. Set EF = ES + activity duration – 1

Moving forward through the network diagram, for each subsequent activity:

3. Set ES = EF + 1 of the preceding activity (if there is more than one preceding activity, use the largest EF + 1)
4. Set EF = ES + activity duration – 1

Using this method, the following calculations are performed:

- For Task ID A:
  - ES = 1 (starts on the first day)
  - EF = ES + activity duration – 1
    = 1 + 2 – 1
    = 2
- For Task ID B:
  - ES = EF + 1 of the largest preceding activity
    = 2 + 1
    = 3
  - EF = ES + activity duration – 1
    = 3 + 10 – 1
    = 12
- For Task ID C:
  - ES = EF + 1 of the largest preceding activity
    = 2 + 1
    = 3
  - EF = ES + activity duration – 1
    = 3 + 1 – 1
    = 3
- For Task ID D:
  - ES = EF + 1 of the largest preceding activity
    = 3 + 1
    = 4
  - EF = ES + activity duration – 1
    = 4 + 1 – 1
    = 4

- For Task ID E:
  - ES = EF + 1 of the largest preceding activity
    - = 12 + 1
    - = 13
  - EF = ES + activity duration – 1
    - = 13 + 1 – 1
    - = 13

On the network diagram, each activity will contain the ES and EF:

Displaying the ES and EF in the Network Diagram

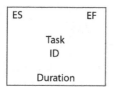

The resulting network diagram is as follows:

Vacation Project with ES and EF

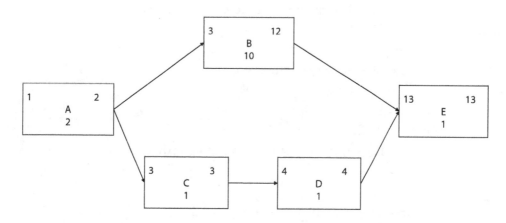

The Backward Pass
The method to calculate the late start (LS) and late finish (LF) of each activity is as follows:

For activities that have no successors (i.e., the final activities in the schedule):
1. Set LF = EF (that was previously calculated in the forward pass)
2. Set LS = LF – activity duration + 1

Moving backward through the network diagram, for each preceding activity:

3. Set LF = LS – 1 of the succeeding activity (if there is more than one succeeding activity, use the smallest LS – 1)
4. Set LS = LF – activity duration + 1

Using this method, the following calculations are performed:

*   For Task ID E:
    *   LF = EF (that was previously calculated in the forward pass)
        = 13
    *   LS = LF – activity duration + 1
        = 13 – 1 + 1
        = 13
*   For Task ID D:
    *   LF = LS – 1 of the smallest succeeding activity
        = 13 – 1
        = 12
    *   LS = LF – activity duration + 1
        = 12 – 1 + 1
        = 12
*   For Task ID C:
    *   LF = LS – 1 of the smallest succeeding activity
        = 12 – 1
        = 11
    *   LS = LF – activity duration + 1
        = 11 – 1 + 1
        = 11
*   For Task ID B:
    *   LF = LS – 1 of the smallest succeeding activity
        = 13 – 1
        = 12
    *   LS = LF – activity duration + 1
        = 12 – 10 + 1
        = 3
*   For Task ID A:
    *   LF = LS – 1 of the smallest succeeding activity
        = 3 – 1
        = 2
    *   LS = LF – activity duration + 1
        = 2 – 2 + 1
        = 1

On the network diagram, each activity will contain the LS and LF:

Displaying the LS and LF in the Network Diagram

ES		EF
	Task ID	
LS	Duration	LF

The resulting network diagram is as follows:

Vacation Project with LS and LF

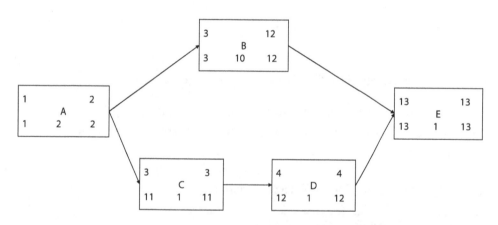

The Total Float

For each activity, the total float is calculated as the difference between the earliest an activity may start/end and the latest an activity may start/end. Therefore:

$$\text{Total Float} = \text{LS} - \text{ES} \qquad \text{OR} \qquad \text{Total Float} = \text{LF} - \text{EF}$$

On the network diagram, each activity will contain the total float:

Displaying the Total Float in the Network Diagram

ES		EF
Total Float	Task ID	
LS	Duration	LF

The resulting calculations are as follows:

Vacation Project with Total Float

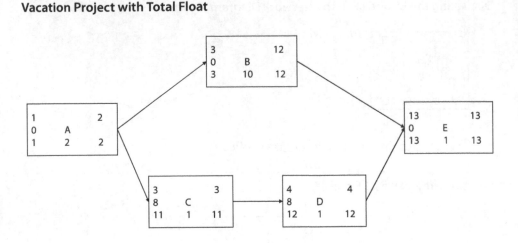

Critical Path Analysis—The Case Study Project

Using the same calculation method, the critical path and total float will be manually calculated for the case study project. In this example, each activity will be assigned a Task ID as follows:

Task IDs for the Case Study Project

Task ID	Activity
A	Initiate the project
B	Plan the project
C	Create sign graphics/text
D	Order banner stands
E	Create holographic cards
F	Order cards
G	Create mural for booth
H	Develop demo slideshow
I	Order mural and tripods
J	Create SM strategy
K	Develop SM post content
L	Update product page

M	Develop online slideshow
N	Create outreach list
O	Perform outreach
P	Create press release
Q	Send press release
R	Develop video concept
S	Develop video storyboard
T	Develop video script
U	Create video
V	Close the project

The Forward Pass

Using the calculation method demonstrated above, the ES and EF may be calculated as follows:

Case Study Network Diagram with ES and EF

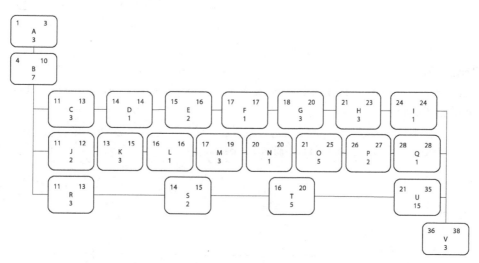

The Backward Pass

Using the calculation method demonstrated above, the LS and LF may be calculated as follows:

Case Study Network Diagram with LS and LF

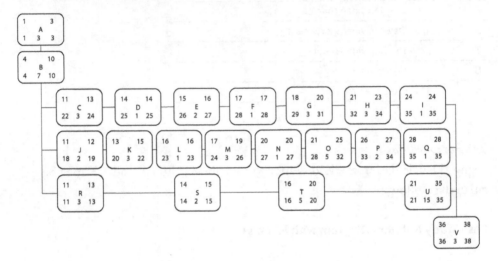

Total Float

Using the calculation method demonstrated above, the total float may be calculated as follows:

Case Study Network Diagram with Total Float

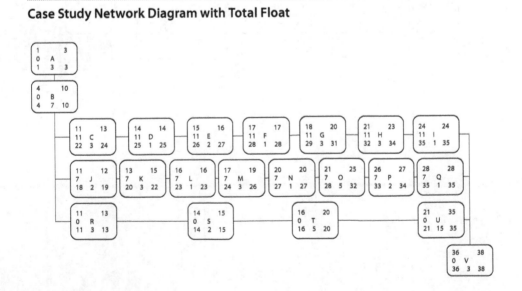

CHAPTER SUMMARY

Key Concepts

1. Using the WBS as a starting point, create an Activity List consisting of one or more activities defined for each work package.
2. Create a project schedule by defining the dependencies between the activities and required activity dates.
3. There are many formats of project schedules, including network diagrams, milestone-driven schedules, activity date-driven schedules, and activity dependency-driven schedules.
4. There are four dependency types: Finish-to-Start, Start-to-Start, Finish-to-Finish, and Start-to-Finish. Start-to-Finish dependency types are rare and are not covered in detail in this text.
5. Activity timing may be affected by the amount of lead or lag defined by the Project Manager.
6. Understanding the critical path allows the Project Manager to determine the total project duration and the impact of activity delays on the project's completion date.

Key Terminology

Activity List: A list of all activities defined for the project.

Activity-Based Schedule: A schedule containing the dates of the activities defined for the project.

Backward Pass: A process that involves moving backward through the project schedule in order to determine the latest date that each task can start and finish.

Baseline: An approved part of the project plan, such as the scope, cost, or schedule. It may be used as a basis for comparison when measuring the progress of the project or considering potential changes to the plan.

Critical Path: The longest sequence of activities in the project schedule. This sequence of activities represents the earliest planned completion time for the project.

Dependency: The required sequence of activities based on the work involved.

Dependency-Based Schedule: A schedule containing the dates and dependencies of the activities defined for the project, often displayed in the Gantt Chart format.

Duration: The total amount of time required to complete an activity. Does not include non-working days such as weekends or holidays.

Early Finish: The earliest time that an activity may finish in a project schedule taking into account the defined dependencies and any other scheduling constraints.

Early Start: The earliest time that an activity may start in a project schedule taking into account the defined dependencies and any other scheduling constraints.

Forward Pass: A process that involves moving forward through the project schedule in order to determine the earliest date that each task can start and finish.

Free Float: The amount of time an activity may be delayed before it delays a subsequent task or the project end date.

Gantt Chart: A chart illustrating the dependencies between activities in a project schedule, where activities are listed in vertical rows and activity durations are represented as horizontal bars.

Lag: The delay or gap of time between two dependent activities.

Late Finish: The latest time that an activity may finish in a project schedule taking into account the defined dependencies and any other scheduling constraints.

Late Start: The latest time that an activity may start in a project schedule taking into account the defined dependencies and any other scheduling constraints.

Lead: The amount of overlap time between two dependent activities.

Milestone: An important event that occurs during a project.

Milestone-Based Schedule: A schedule containing the dates of the milestones defined for the project.

Network Diagram: A graph that demonstrates the sequence of activities during the project. Activities are represented as rectangles, and dependencies between activities are represented as lines.

Total Float: The amount of time an activity may be delayed before it delays the project end date.

Work-Back Schedule: A specific type of activity-based schedule in which the timing of each activity is determined by working backward from the project's end date.

DISCUSSION QUESTIONS

1. Consider the purchase of a new product that you may be planning over the next year (e.g., phone, vacation). Make a list of the activities that are needed to complete this purchase.

2. For the list of activities identified above, arrange them into a logical order. Are there any activities that can be performed in parallel?

3. The duration of an activity can be difficult to estimate. What are the factors that could cause the duration of an activity to be difficult to predict?

4. There are three types of schedules that are defined in this chapter: the milestone-driven schedule, the activity date-driven schedule, and the activity dependency-driven schedule. What are some of the factors that would cause a Project Manager to choose to use each of these schedule types during a project?

5. Provide an everyday example that demonstrates a finish-to-start, start-to-start, and finish-to-finish dependency.

6. Perform an online search to research project scheduling challenges. Based on your findings, what are some of the challenges encountered during the scheduling process?

Budget Planning

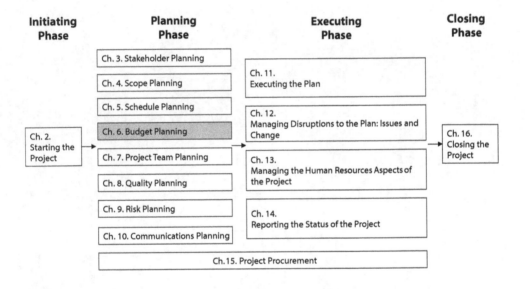

Initiating Phase	Planning Phase	Executing Phase	Closing Phase

- Ch. 3. Stakeholder Planning
- Ch. 4. Scope Planning
- Ch. 5. Schedule Planning
- Ch. 6. Budget Planning
- Ch. 7. Project Team Planning
- Ch. 8. Quality Planning
- Ch. 9. Risk Planning
- Ch. 10. Communications Planning

Ch. 2. Starting the Project

Ch. 11. Executing the Plan

Ch. 12. Managing Disruptions to the Plan: Issues and Change

Ch. 13. Managing the Human Resources Aspects of the Project

Ch. 14. Reporting the Status of the Project

Ch. 15. Project Procurement

Ch. 16. Closing the Project

INTRODUCTION TO BUDGET PLANNING

After planning the project scope and schedule, it is now time to plan for the cost of the project.

Project Sponsors and other key stakeholders tend to focus on project costs because of the impact of cost overruns. Higher project costs may have one or more of the following impacts:

- Reduction of the project's Business Case justification, leading to the cancellation of the project.
- Deferral of other projects due to reduced availability of funding.
- Reduction of the company's profit (in for-profit organizations) or increased deficits and/or tax increases (in government or not-for-profit organizations).

Given these impacts, it is very important to carefully plan the project's costs. This helps ensure that the project's budget is consistent with the planned project scope and schedule, and also enables the costs to be managed effectively throughout the project.

There are two main steps when planning for project cost:

Budget Planning

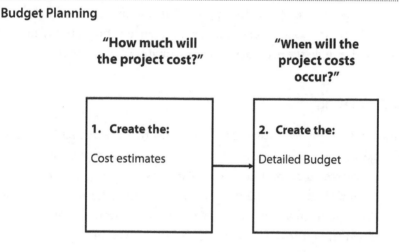

During the first step, cost estimates are created for all aspects of the project. Next, the estimates are distributed over the timeline of the project.

HOW MUCH WILL THE PROJECT COST?

During the Initiating Phase, the overall budget for the project is added to the Project Charter. The budget amount tends to be a general estimate, often developed during the creation of the Business Case. Alternatively, it may represent the funds that are available for the project. During the Planning Phase, the costs of the project are estimated in detail, based on the deliverables to be produced during the project.

Costs occur during a project for a variety of reasons. Some are direct costs, meaning that they occur directly because of the activities of the project. Often the most significant direct cost results from the amount of **work** performed. Other direct costs include the materials that are purchased, equipment that is purchased or rented, and travel costs. There may also be indirect costs, such as the cost of the company's facilities (e.g., rent and utilities), employee benefits, and office supplies used by the project team. There are various approaches that may be used to develop cost estimates.

Analogous Estimating

Analogous Estimating involves developing an estimate based on the cost that was incurred during a previous, similar project. The advantage of this method is that it is very easy to perform and can be done early in the planning phase. The disadvantage is that previous cost information is required, which may not be available for each project. Therefore, this approach is not always possible. There is also the risk that differences between the past and current project may not be known, which could reduce the accuracy of the estimate.

Parametric Estimating

Parametric Estimating involves using standard rates that are available for certain types of project activities as a basis for estimating. For example, when planning a banquet, a caterer may provide a per plate cost for their services. This unit cost is then multiplied by the planned attendance in order to develop the estimate. The advantage of this approach is that it is an accurate method of cost estimating. The disadvantage is that it may only be used for certain types of costs where standard rates are available.

Bottom-up Estimating

Bottom-up Estimating involves assessing the characteristics of each work package in the WBS and Project Scope Statement and then estimating the costs related to each work package. This is the most detailed form of estimating. The advantage of this approach is that it tends to be a relatively accurate form of cost estimating given the high level of detail. The disadvantage is that it requires detailed scope and schedule information and therefore this type of estimate may not be produced until later in the Planning Phase. The quality of the detailed estimates also depends on the expertise of the estimator.

Case Study Update: Creating the Cost Estimates

For Sophie, creating the cost estimates is the trickiest part of the business. From past experience, she has learned that estimating too high could cause projects to be cancelled, but estimating too low could mean she would exceed her costs later. A "guesstimate" is simply not good enough.

This time, Sophie feels more confident. Thanks to her earlier work brainstorming and categorizing the work packages, she can now better assess the estimated costs of each work package and therefore the overall project.

Sophie decides that to perform this task, a change of scenery is in order. On the way to work, she pulls into the parking lot of her local coffee shop. After ordering a large coffee, she opens her laptop and looks at the project schedule. The majority of the costs for this project will come from the people working on the project in the form of their salaries. At Deco Productions, the Finance department has calculated what is known as a "loaded rate" for employees who work on projects. This loaded rate is an hourly rate that includes not only their salaries, but also reflects overhead costs, such as benefits, building costs, and office supplies. So far, two people have been assigned to the project: Sophie (Project Manager) and Jason Brown (a Business Analyst who worked on the scope planning activities). The loaded rates for these two project roles are:

- Project Manager $100/hour
- Business Analyst $80/hour

While other team members have not yet been assigned to the project, based on the work involved, Sophie knows she will need the following:

- Graphic Designer $50/hour
- Communications Specialist $60/hour
- Marketing Specialist $60/hour
- Videographer $50/hour

For each activity, she considers the amount of work that will be required. For some activities, she uses her in-depth knowledge of the work involved, while for others, she considers past projects. For the graphics-related work, she makes a quick call to one of the company's graphic designers to verify her estimates.

Sophie also includes the cost of her own time and that of Jason, the Business Analyst, which she predicts will be spent during the Executing Phase. During the five weeks of execution, she estimates that about one-third of her time will be needed to manage the team, resolve issues, and communicate with the project stakeholders. She also estimates that she will need about one day per week of Jason's time to answer the project team's questions about the project scope and provide quality control for the completed deliverables.

Next, Sophie creates a list that contains the amount of materials and equipment that the project will need:

- Trade show banner stands (5)
- Holographic cards for the trade show booth (2,000)

Continued

- Murals for the multimedia demo (2)
- Camera and tripods for the multimedia demo (2)

As she records this information, she checks the current price of each item listed on a number of suppliers' websites. Finally, she considers any additional costs that may be incurred during the project.

One hour, one large coffee, and two maple donuts later, Sophie has settled on a total cost estimate for the project and heads into work.

The following are the cost estimates produced for the project:

Cost Estimates

HUMAN RESOURCES COST ESTIMATES					
Activity	**Duration (days)**	**Resource**	**% Allo-cated**	**Daily Rate**	**Cost**
Initiating Phase					
Initiate the project	3	Project Manager	50%	$800.00	$1,200.00
Total Initiating Phase					**$1,200.00**
Planning Phase					
Plan the project	7	Project Manager	50%	$800.00	$2,800.00
	7	Business Analyst	100%	$640.00	$4,480.00
Total Planning Phase					**$7,280.00**
Executing Phase					
Create sign graphics/ text	3	Graphic Designer	100%	$400.00	$1,200.00
Order banner stands	1	Graphic Designer	100%	$400.00	$400.00
Create holographic cards	2	Graphic Designer	100%	$400.00	$800.00
Order cards	1	Graphic Designer	100%	$400.00	$400.00
Create mural for booth	3	Graphic Designer	100%	$400.00	$1,200.00
Develop demo slideshow	3	Graphic Designer	100%	$400.00	$1,200.00
Order mural and tripods	1	Graphic Designer	100%	$400.00	$400.00
Create SM strategy	2	Communications Specialist	100%	$480.00	$960.00
Develop SM post content	3	Communications Specialist	100%	$480.00	$1,440.00

Update product page	1	Communications Specialist	100%	$480.00	$480.00
Develop online slideshow	3	Communications Specialist	100%	$480.00	$1,440.00
Create outreach list	1	Communications Specialist	100%	$480.00	$480.00
Perform outreach	5	Communications Specialist	100%	$480.00	$2,400.00
Create press release	2	Communications Specialist	100%	$480.00	$960.00
Send press release	1	Communications Specialist	100%	$480.00	$480.00
Develop video concept	3	Marketing Specialist	100%	$480.00	$1,440.00
Develop video storyboard	2	Marketing Specialist	100%	$480.00	$960.00
Develop video script	5	Marketing Specialist	100%	$480.00	$2,400.00
Create video	15	Videographer	100%	$400.00	$6,000.00
	15	Marketing Specialist	100%	$480.00	$7,200.00
Monitoring and Controlling	25	Project Manager	34%	$800.00	$6,800.00
	25	Business Analyst	20%	$640.00	$3,200.00
Total Executing Phase					**$42,240.00**
Closing Phase					
Close the project	3	Project Manager	50%	$800.00	$1,200.00
Total Closing Phase					**$1,200.00**
Total HR Cost Estimates					**$51,920.00**

Other Cost Estimates

Item	Quantity	Description	Unit Cost	Cost
Banner stands	5	Banner stands for trades show	$200.00	$1,000.00
Holographic cards	2,000	Cards for trade show booth giveaways	$1.00	$2,000.00
Murals	2	Murals for trade show multimedia demo	$100.00	$200.00
Camera and tripod	2	Camera and tripod for trade show multimedia demo	$700.00	$1,400.00
Total Other Cost Estimates				**$4,600.00**
Total Project Cost Estimates				**$56,520.00**

Once the detailed estimates are created for the project, they should be compared to the budget for the project that was documented in the Project Charter. In the case study, the detailed estimate is less than the original budget amount. This is a desirable position to be in at this point in the project. During the project, actual costs may increase by up to $3,480 before the original budget is exceeded. This is known as a **budget contingency**.

If the detailed estimates exceed the Project Charter budget, discussions with the Project Sponsor would need to take place. Possible solutions include modifying the project scope and/or increasing the funds available to the project. If any changes occur, the Project Charter would need to be updated, as well as the WBS, Project Scope Statement, and project schedule.

WHEN WILL THE PROJECT COSTS OCCUR?

In order to accurately plan for the timing of project costs, an activity-based schedule (i.e., an activity date-driven schedule or activity dependency-driven schedule) is required. The processes described in this section would generally be performed for projects with a long duration and/or high costs. For projects with short durations and/or low costs, this level of cost planning is generally not required.

Case Study Update: Creating the Detailed Budget

Sophie reviews the total cost estimate of the project. She is relieved that it is less than the $60,000 budget, giving her a small contingency fund. However, she also knows from experience that costs often are higher than estimated and they will need to be managed closely throughout the project.

To do so, in addition to the amount of the estimated costs, she will need to know when they are planned to occur. For example, if $30,000 is spent by the halfway point of the project, does this mean that the project will meet its budget? What if more of the costs will be incurred near the end of the project? This could indicate that the project will be over budget.

Opening her laptop, Sophie creates a spreadsheet as follows:

- For each row, she lists each phase of the project (Initiating, Planning, Executing, Closing). Within each phase, she creates a row for the HR costs and other non-HR costs (if there are any for the phase).
- For each column, she lists each week of the project (eight in total).

Using the project schedule and the planned costs that are contained in the detailed estimates, she begins to fill in the cells of the spreadsheet.

For example, for the week ending March 27th, her calculations would be as follows:

- The "initiate the project" activity is planned to start and finish in three days. The Project Manager (Sophie) plans to spend 50% of her time on this activity. Because her daily rate is $800, this results in a total planned cost of $1,200 ($400/day × 3 days). This amount is placed under the March 27th column for HR Costs in the Initiating Phase.

- The first two days of the "plan the project" activity is also planned to start during this week. There are two resources assigned to this activity: 50% of the Project Manager's and 100% of the Business Analyst's time. This results in a total planned cost of $2,080 ($400/day × 2 days for the Project Manager + $640/day × 2 for the Business Analyst).

Sophie continues to calculate the planned cost for each of the remaining seven weeks of the project schedule. For the non-HR costs, she determines when these costs will likely occur. Based on the schedule, the banner stands ($1,000) will be ordered during the week ending April 10th, the cards ($2,000) during the week ending April 17th, and the cameras and tripods during the week ending April 24th. All of these costs will occur during the Executing Phase.

Once complete, she double-checks her work to ensure that the total cost in her new spreadsheet ($56,520) matches the total of the cost estimates that she developed earlier. Once the planned costs for all weeks are calculated, the Detailed Budget is complete.

The following is the **Detailed Budget** for the case study project:

Detailed Budget (Weekly)

DETAILED BUDGET									
Project Name	DCV4Launch–DecoCam V4 Product Launch								
Cost Category	Week ending 27-Mar	Week ending 3-Apr	Week ending 10-Apr	Week ending 17-Apr	Week ending 24-Apr	Week ending 1-May	Week ending 8-May	Week ending 15-May	Total
Initiating									
HR costs	$1,200								$1,200
Planning									
HR costs	$2,080	$5,200							$7,280

Continued

Executing									
HR costs			$8,800	$8,800	$10,400	$7,840	$6,400		$42,240
Other costs			$1,000	$2,000	$1,600				$4,600
Closing									
HR costs								$1,200	$1,200
Total Costs	**$3,280**	**$5,200**	**$9,800**	**$10,800**	**$12,000**	**$7,840**	**$6,400**	**$1,200**	**$56,520**

While every project will have its own unique distribution of costs, the Detailed Budget shown above is typical of how costs are incurred during a project. In the early stage of the project (Week 1, above), costs are relatively low. This corresponds to the Initiating Phase. Costs tend to increase during the Planning Phase and the start of the Executing Phase (Weeks 2 and 3). As the Executing Phase continues (Weeks 4 to 7), the costs continue to rise rapidly, peaking at about the three-fourths point of the project and then beginning to fall as the work nears completion. During the Closing Phase (Week 8), the costs are relatively low.

When creating a Detailed Budget, two decisions need to be made:

- The cost categories need to be determined: in the case study, the costs are broken down by project phase and then by HR costs and other costs within each phase. The costs could also have been broken down by work package or activity.
- The time periods for each column need to be determined: since the total project duration is just under eight weeks in the case study, the decision was made that each column would represent one week of the project. For longer projects, each column may be defined as a month or a quarter (three months).

In order to make the above decisions, the Project Manager would need to determine the required level of cost information required for the project, bearing in mind that the greater the level of detail, the more work will be required to create and maintain the Detailed Budget.

As an example, if the decision were made to structure the Detailed Budget by monthly costs, it would appear as follows:

Detailed Budget (Monthly)

DETAILED BUDGET				
Project Name	DCV4Launch–DecoCam V4 Product Launch			
Cost Category	**March**	**April**	**May**	**Total**
Initiating				
HR costs	$1,200			**$1,200**
Planning				
HR costs	$4,160	$3,120		**$7,280**
Executing				
HR costs		$34,560	$7,680	**$42,240**
Other costs		$4,600		**$4,600**
Closing				
HR costs			$1,200	**$1,200**
Total Costs	**$5,360**	**$42,280**	**$8,880**	**$56,520**

There are many benefits of creating a Detailed Budget, including the following:

- Management of project costs: as actual project costs are incurred during the project, they may be compared to the planned costs. This leads to more effective management of project costs, as potential cost overages are more likely to be detected earlier in the project.
- Knowledge of the required cash flow: this budget demonstrates the timing of expenses. For example, in the Detailed Budget, the timing of other expenses (e.g., murals, cards, cameras, and tripods) can be easily determined.

CHAPTER SUMMARY

Key Concepts

1. Develop cost estimates for the human resources, materials, equipment, and other requirements.
2. Create a project budget that shows the distribution of the estimated costs over the timeline of the project.

Key Terminology

Analogous Estimate: An estimate based on the cost that was incurred during a previous, similar project.

Bottom-up Estimate: An estimate based on the characteristics of each work package in the WBS and Project Scope Statement.

Budget Contingency: The difference between the total approved Project Budget and the current cost estimate.

Detailed Budget: A planning document showing the timing of all planned costs for the project.

Parametric Estimate: An estimate based on the availability of standard rates that are used as a basis for estimating.

Work: The actual amount of time spent on an activity.

DISCUSSION QUESTIONS

1. Think of a project from your personal, work, or school activities where the actual costs incurred were higher than you originally anticipated. Describe the reasons why your cost estimates were inaccurate.

2. Provide an example where each of the three estimating techniques—analogous, parametric, and bottom-up—would be appropriate.

3. In order to ensure the project does not go over budget, a Project Manager doubles the cost estimates. What are the potential problems that this approach may create?

4. Perform an online search to research different reasons for cost overruns. Based on your findings, summarize the five most common reasons for cost overruns.

7 Project Team Planning

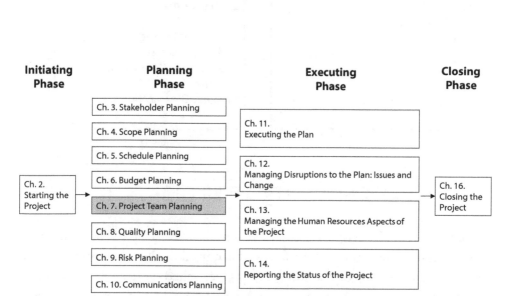

Initiating Phase	Planning Phase	Executing Phase	Closing Phase
	Ch. 3. Stakeholder Planning		
	Ch. 4. Scope Planning	Ch. 11. Executing the Plan	
	Ch. 5. Schedule Planning		
Ch. 2. Starting the Project	Ch. 6. Budget Planning	Ch. 12. Managing Disruptions to the Plan: Issues and Change	Ch. 16. Closing the Project
	Ch. 7. Project Team Planning	Ch. 13. Managing the Human Resources Aspects of the Project	
	Ch. 8. Quality Planning		
	Ch. 9. Risk Planning	Ch. 14. Reporting the Status of the Project	
	Ch. 10. Communications Planning		
	Ch. 15. Project Procurement		

INTRODUCTION TO PROJECT TEAM PLANNING

During the planning for the project schedule, the number and skills of the people required for the project were identified. These included a Business Analyst, Graphic Designer, Communications Specialist, Marketing Specialist, and Videographer. Other than the Business Analyst, the rest of the team had not yet been assigned to the project.

During the next stage of project planning, the processes to plan for the project team members will be examined. When planning for the project team, it is useful to think of the project as a temporary organization that happens to reside within a permanent organization. It will need an organizational structure, an ability to bring people into and out of the temporary organization, and roles for the team members to perform.

There are two main steps when planning for project human resources:

Project Team Planning

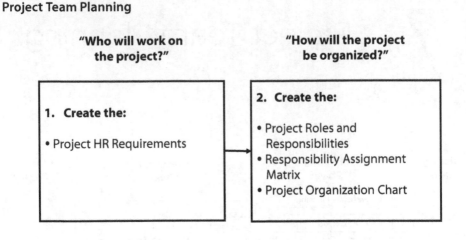

WHO WILL WORK ON THE PROJECT?

Once the Project Manager is assigned to a project, a key task is to ensure that project team members are identified and acquired during the project. Up to this point in the project planning, the project schedule has been developed by estimating the human resources and work effort needed for each activity. Putting this information together, the resource needs on a week-by-week basis may be determined.

Human resources are generally acquired from the following three sources:
- Internal (already employed by the organization)
- New hires (to be hired by the organization in order to work on the project)
- Contract workers (to be hired on contract to work on the project)

The use of internal human resources involves acquiring team members for a certain period of time as required by the project. They may be assigned to the project full-time or for a certain percentage of their time.

In some cases, the human resources required for a project are not available within the organization. One option is to hire a new employee or multiple employees to work on the project. Given the amount of time needed to hire a new employee (weeks or in some cases even months), a great deal of lead time is necessary to ensure new hires are available when needed for a project.

A third source of human resources is contract workers who are brought into the organization in order to work on the project. Depending on the type of human resources required, the amount of lead time may vary. For example, lower skill/abundant human resources may be acquired in a few days, while higher skill/less abundant human resources may be acquired in a few weeks or more. Each of the above approaches has advantages and disadvantages.

Internal staff members are more likely to be familiar with the organization and be known to the Project Manager. The experience gained during the project will stay within the organization and may be applied to future projects. However, there is a limited number of internal staff and they may be allocated to other projects. Additionally, they may not possess the skill level necessary for the project.

New hires can provide the organization with the opportunity to acquire new skill sets for the project and they also increase the number of potential resources available to the project. The downside is the long lead time of the hiring process. The new hire will also be unfamiliar with the organization, which can result in taking a longer amount of time to become productive during the project.

Contract workers increase the number of potential resources available to the project and can generally be acquired more quickly than new hires. However, they may be unfamiliar with the organization and the experience gained by the contract worker will leave the organization once their time on the project ends.

The human resources required for a project may be acquired either by the Project Manager, a Resource Manager, or combination of both. A Resource Manager is a person within an organization whose responsibilities include acquiring the human resources needed for projects.

Case Study Update: Creating the Project HR Requirements

As Sophie develops the project schedule, she naturally begins to think about the human resources needs of her project. Deco Productions always has a number of overlapping projects underway at any one point in time, so it can be challenging to get the workers she wants assigned to her project.

In the Deco Productions organization, all of the project workers report to a Resource Manager (Adrian Binkley). Adrian's responsibility is to work with each Project Manager to ensure that each project receives the human resources necessary to complete their project. This is a very challenging process, as each project often requires the same type of human resources at the same time. This often involves a great deal of discussion, negotiation, and, in some cases, adjustments to the project timeline.

Continued

Sophie knows from experience that in order to ensure Adrian assigns the required human resources to her project, she needs to demonstrate when she needs each type of resource. It is no longer sufficient to talk generally about when team members are required. With the company's increased focus on cost reduction, Sophie is expected to provide spreadsheets detailing her resource needs. She opens her laptop and examines her schedule. Looking at each week of the schedule, she notes the human resources time required and records this information into a resource spreadsheet.

Once complete, Sophie sends Adrian a link to the spreadsheet and then heads to his office. After her detailed planning, she is feeling good about their meeting.

The following is the **Project HR Requirements** for the case study project:

Project HR Requirements

PROJECT HR REQUIREMENTS								
Project Name	DCV4Launch–DecoCam V4 Product Launch							
Resource Type	**Week ending 27-Mar**	**Week ending 3-Apr**	**Week ending 10-Apr**	**Week ending 17-Apr**	**Week ending 24-Apr**	**Week ending 1-May**	**Week ending 8-May**	**Week ending 15-May**
Project Manager	2.5 days	2.5 days	1.7 days	1.7 days	1.7 days	1.7 days	1.7 days	1.5 days
Business Analyst	2 days	5 days	1 day	1 day	1 day	1 day	1 day	
Graphic Designer			5 days	5 days	4 days			
Communications Specialist			5 days	5 days	5 days	3 days		
Marketing Specialist			5 days	5 days	5 days	5 days	5 days	
Videographer			5 days	5 days	5 days	5 days	5 days	

HOW WILL THE PROJECT BE ORGANIZED?

Project Roles and Responsibilities

As human resources are acquired, the project team begins to form. It is important that each team member understands their role on the project and their project responsibilities. Therefore, the roles and responsibilities of each team member should be documented.

The following is the **Project Roles and Responsibilities** template:

Project Roles and Responsibilities Template

PROJECT ROLES AND RESPONSIBILITIES		
Project Name	[This section contains the project name that should appear consistently on all project documents. Organizations often have project naming conventions.]	
Name	**Role**	**Responsibilities**
[Team member name.]	[Their role or job title.]	[Detailed description of their project responsibilities and job duties.]

Case Study Update: Creating the Project Roles and Responsibilities

Leaving Adrian's office, Sophie feels good about the people who have been assigned to her project. As expected, Jason Brown will continue through the Executing Phase of the project. Chris Sandburg is assigned to be the Graphic Designer. Sophie has had a good working relationship with Chris over the years so this is a big plus for the project. A relatively new employee, Sarah Pierce, is assigned to be the project's Communications Specialist. Sophie is less familiar with her, but she thinks it will work out well. Another plus is the assignment of Maddy Wen as the Marketing Specialist for the project. Sophie perceives that the one potential negative assignment to the project is that of Eli Briggs as the project's Videographer. Eli has been a challenge to work with on past projects. Sophie makes a mental note to find ways to motivate Eli during this project.

Now that her team is in place, Sophie begins to document the key responsibilities of each team member. Since many of the responsibilities are inherent in the role and do not vary significantly from project to project, she is able to use previous Roles and Responsibilities documents from other projects as a starting point. However, as each project is unique, she ensures that any additional or modified responsibilities are included.

The following is the Roles and Responsibilities document for the case study project:

Project Roles and Responsibilities

PROJECT ROLES AND RESPONSIBILITIES		
Project Name	DCV4Launch–DecoCam V4 Product Launch	
Name	**Role**	**Responsibilities**
Arun Singh	Project Sponsor	• Provides funding for the project. • Provides overall direction and approves major changes for the project. • Provides final sign off for the project. • Communicates the project's progress to the senior management of Deco Productions.
Sophie Featherstone	Project Manager	• Overall responsibility for the project's completion. • Creates and maintains the project plans. • Approves minor changes and determines which changes will require Project Sponsor approval. • Manages the project team and assists each team member to resolve issues. • Communicates project updates and other information to the Project Sponsor.
Jason Brown	Business Analyst	• Completes the project scope-related documents. • Communicates project updates and any issues to the Project Manager. • Clarifies the project scope to the project team as requested. • Performs quality control for all completed deliverables.
Chris Sandburg	Graphic Designer	• Responsible for the completion of all work packages related to the trade show. • Communicates project updates and any issues to the Project Manager. • Provides graphic design consulting to the rest of the project team as required.
Sarah Pierce	Communications Specialist	• Responsible for the completion of all work packages related to media relations, social media, and updates to the website. • Communicates project updates and any issues to the Project Manager. • Provides communications consulting to the rest of the project team as required.
Maddy Wen	Marketing Specialist	• Responsible for the completion of the promotional video. • Provides direction to the Videographer. • Communicates project updates and any issues to the Project Manager. • Provides marketing consulting to the rest of the project team as required.

Eli Briggs	Videographer	• Responsible for the completion of video-related activities under the direction of the Marketing Specialist. • Communicates project updates and any issues to the Marketing Specialist.

Responsibility Assignment Matrix

Another planning tool that may be used to clarify the planned involvement of people within the project is known as a **Responsibility Assignment Matrix** (RAM).

One type of RAM is known as an **RACI Chart**. The acronym RACI stands for Responsible, Accountable, Consulted, and Informed. The template is as follows:

RACI Chart Template

RACI CHART							
	[Name]	[Name]	[Name]	[Name]	[Name]	[Name]	[Name]
[Project work package or activity.]	R/A/C/I	R/A/C/I	R/A/C/I	R/A/C/I	R/A/C/I	R/A/C/I	R/A/C/I
R–Responsible A–Accountable C–Consulted I–Informed							

An RACI Chart contains the following four codes that are used to describe each person's involvement in the project:

- R–Responsible: a person who will actually perform the work
- A–Accountable: a person who will ensure the work is completed successfully
- C–Consulted: a person who will have input into the work being performed; those responsible for the work would normally consult with this person
- I–Informed: a person who will be informed regarding the work

Case Study Update: Creating the Responsibility Assignment Matrix

Sophie calls her new project team together to discuss the project and their roles. While the Roles and Responsibilities document is very informative to the team, the team members have additional questions, such as "do I need to let anyone know when I'm done my work?" and "who makes sure that work is complete?"

Continued

To help clarify this information, Sophie leads a discussion with the team. Using the RACI Chart, she places the Project Sponsor and the names of each project team member at the top of each column. For each high-level deliverable, the team discusses who should make sure the work is completed, who should complete the work, who should be consulted, and who should be informed.

RACI Charts may be developed at any level of detail, either for the entire project or for subsets of the project. For the case study project, it was developed for each high-level deliverable.

RACI Chart

RACI CHART							
	Arun	Sophie	Jason	Chris	Sarah	Maddy	Eli
Trade Show Support	C	C	C	A,R	I	I	I
Communications	C	C	C	I	A,R	I	I
Promotional Video	C	C	C	I	I	A,R	R
Project Management	C	A,R	C	I	I	I	I

R–Responsible A–Accountable C–Consulted I–Informed

An RACI Chart provides useful information to the people working on the project. For example, the above RACI Chart illustrates the following regarding the Promotional Video deliverable:

- Maddy will be held accountable to make sure the video is completed according to the schedule and will also perform the work (responsible).
- Eli will perform the work under Maddy's direction (responsible).
- Sophie, Jason, and Arun will be consulted as required.
- Chris and Sarah will be kept aware (informed) of the work during the project.

For the management of the project, Sophie is responsible for the following:
- She is both accountable to ensure it is performed and also performs the work (responsible).
- She will consult with Jason and Arun as required.
- She will inform the rest of the project team of the progress of the project.

Project Organization Chart

Companies often create hierarchical charts to demonstrate their internal organization. For example, a company organization chart may list each department and the people who work in them. This helps stakeholders understand how the work of the company is being performed as well as the roles and relationships of the team members.

As projects can be considered temporary organizations that exist within companies, it can be useful to create a **Project Organization Chart** for the same reasons.

Here is the organization chart for the case study project:

Project Organization Chart

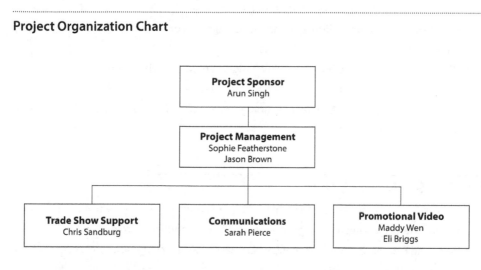

This Project Organization Chart demonstrates the following organizational information:

- At the top of the chart is Arun, the Project Sponsor, who has overall accountability for the project.
- Reporting to Arun is Sophie, the Project Manager, who is accountable for the management of the project. Jason, the Business Analyst, reports to Sophie.
- There are three main parts of the project—Trade Show Support, Communications, and the Promotional Video. The team member(s) are listed for each.

CHAPTER SUMMARY

Key Concepts

1. Acquire the human resources needed to complete the project.
2. Organize the project team to ensure that their accountabilities are clear and understood.

Key Terminology

Project HR Requirements: A planning document indicating the type of human resources needed and the amount of time they are required for a project.

Project Organization Chart: A hierarchical chart that demonstrates the organization of the project and how the areas of responsibility interrelate.

Project Roles and Responsibilities: A planning document containing a description of the key project roles.

RACI Chart: A specific type of Responsibility Assignment Matrix. The acronym RACI stands for Responsible, Accountable, Consulted, and Informed.

Responsibility Assignment Matrix: A planning tool used to clarify the planned involvement of people within the project.

DISCUSSION QUESTIONS

1. Think of a project from your personal, work, or school activities in which people working on the project were disorganized or confused about their role. Describe how the Roles and Responsibilities document, RACI Chart, or Project Organization Chart may have helped during this project.
2. Perform an online search to research the following question: "How long does the hiring process take?" According to your findings, what is the average length of time of the hiring process? What are the implications of this when planning for human resources on a project?
3. The Roles and Responsibilities document and the Responsibility Assignment Matrix are both used to define the responsibilities of the project team. Describe how these two documents differ.
4. Should the Project Manager be involved in the acquisition of new team members or should this be left to the Resource Manager?

8 Quality Planning

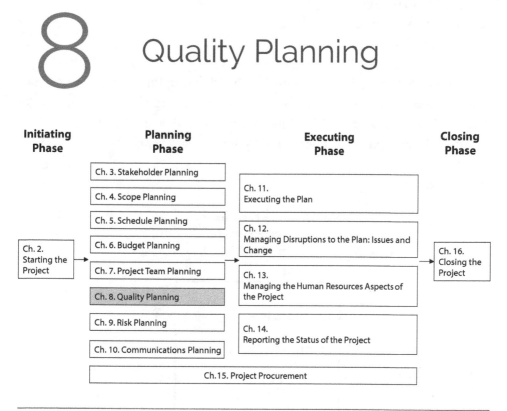

Initiating Phase	Planning Phase	Executing Phase	Closing Phase

Ch. 3. Stakeholder Planning

Ch. 4. Scope Planning

Ch. 11. Executing the Plan

Ch. 5. Schedule Planning

Ch. 2. Starting the Project

Ch. 6. Budget Planning

Ch. 12. Managing Disruptions to the Plan: Issues and Change

Ch. 7. Project Team Planning

Ch. 16. Closing the Project

Ch. 13. Managing the Human Resources Aspects of the Project

Ch. 8. Quality Planning

Ch. 9. Risk Planning

Ch. 14. Reporting the Status of the Project

Ch. 10. Communications Planning

Ch. 15. Project Procurement

INTRODUCTION TO QUALITY PLANNING

Project **quality** is closely associated with the scope of a project. While the scope indicates what a project will produce, its quality is measured by how the product of the project performs. J. M. Juran and J. A. De Feo (2010) define quality as follows: "To be fit for purpose, every good and service must have the right features to satisfy the customer needs and must be delivered with few failures."[1]

A key theme of quality management is that quality should be designed into the product rather than relying on inspection to find defects. W. Edwards Deming (2000) argued that "quality comes not from inspection, but from improvement of the production process."[2] The focus of project quality management should be on the development of sound processes from the start of the project and throughout all of its phases. The greater the focus placed on improving the ongoing processes of the project, the less inspection and rework required. For this reason, an important aspect of quality management is promoting a culture of continuous improvement at both the organization and project level.

Quality management consists of the following three main categories:

1. Quality Planning
2. Quality Assurance
3. Quality Control

Quality Planning takes place during the Planning Phase of the project and will be covered in this chapter. Quality Assurance and Quality Control take place during the Executing Phase and will be covered later in the text.

There is one main step when planning for project quality:

Quality Planning

"What are the quality standards for the project?"

1. Create the:

Quality Management Plan

WHAT ARE THE QUALITY STANDARDS FOR THE PROJECT?

When planning for project quality, the two main functions outlined in Juran and De Feo's (2010) definition—the necessity to have "features to satisfy the customer needs" and "few failures"— should be considered more closely.

Success in developing features to satisfy the customer needs relies to a large extent on the scope planning processes covered in Chapter 4. As discussed, gathering the customer's requirements and defining the scope of the project accurately are key to satisfying the customer's needs.

The second part of the definition involves determining if the product is free from deficiencies and performs as expected. In order to do so, it is important to define what is expected of the product. A **standard** is a level or grade that may be used as a measure of quality.

For example, consider the press release that will be created as part of the case study project. One of the standards for press releases is that they must follow The Canadian Press (CP) style.

Another standard for press releases is in regards to their length. The standard length of a press release is 250 words. However, since it is unlikely that all press releases will reach this exact word count, a **tolerance** is permitted. Tolerance is the maximum allowable variance from the standard or specifications of the project. If a tolerance of 50 words is defined, then a press release that has between 200 and 300 words would meet the standard, while a press release of 180 words or 320 words would not.

The case above demonstrates the use of **metrics**. Metrics are numerical values that are used to make objective quality measurements. For example, determining whether a numerical standard of 250 words has been met is more effective than trying to meet a more general standard, such as writing a press release of "moderate length."

Quality Management Plans describe the organization's policy on quality, the quality-related roles in the organization, and any other quality-related information. The content of the Quality Management Plan for this text focuses on defining the quality standards for the project.

The Quality Management Plan template is shown below:

Quality Management Plan Template

QUALITY MANAGEMENT PLAN	
Project Name	[This section contains the project name that should appear consistently on all project documents. Organizations often have project naming conventions.]
Quality Standards	

[Category Standards]

1. [Standard #1]
2. [Standard #2]
3. [Standard #3]

[Category Standards]

1. [Standard #4]
2. [Standard #5]
3. [Standard #6]

Case Study Update: Creating the Quality Management Plan

Now that her project team planning is complete, Sophie turns to her attention to the next element of the plan: project quality. She starts by asking herself a simple question: "How will quality be achieved for this project?"

She sets out to list the features that will set the project apart and help ensure that it is a quality project. Given the creation of graphics and videos, there is a fair amount of technology involved. Sophie knows that technology failures tend to reflect on the overall project quality, even if they are minor. So, she begins by writing "Technical Standards" on a sheet of paper.

Next, she considers the amount of written text that will be produced, such as the press release, holographic cards, the mural, and updates to the website. Since even a single spelling or grammar error reduces the perception of quality, she writes "Writing Standards" as another subheading on the sheet.

Sophie knows that social media will be used significantly during the product launch. This is something that can be of great benefit to the project but can also be detrimental if mistakes are made. She adds "Social Media Standards" to the sheet.

And finally, she knows how important communication is to the success and quality of the project. She writes "Communication Standards" as the last subheading.

For each subheading, she starts to list the standards that should be met for the project. In some cases, the standards are defined by the Deco Productions organization, while the others are standards defined for this project.

The following is the Quality Management Plan for the case study project:

Quality Management Plan

QUALITY MANAGEMENT PLAN	
Project Name	DCV4Launch–DecoCam V4 Product Launch
Quality Standards	

Technical Standards
1. All image files will be in the company standard file type and will meet the standard minimum resolution.
2. All video files will be in the company standard file type and will meet the standard minimum resolution.
3. All images displayed must be verified to ensure that there is no copyright infringement.

Writing Standards
1. The press release will use CP style.
2. The press release will be 250 words, with a tolerance of plus or minus 50 words.
3. All written material that will be viewed by anyone outside of the company will contain zero spelling or grammatical errors.

Social Media Standards

1. All social media content produced will meet the company's Social Media Policy in terms of content, frequency, and approved social media platforms.

Communication Standards

1. All emails must be responded to within 24 hours.
2. Meeting agendas for all formal project meetings are required 24 hours in advance of the meeting.
3. Minutes are required for all formal project meetings within 48 hours of the meeting completion.
4. The status of the project (updated schedule and budget) must be reported to the Project Sponsor on a weekly basis.

CHAPTER SUMMARY

Key Concepts

1. To achieve quality, the product or service must have the right features to satisfy the customer's needs and be delivered with few failures.
2. Quality should be designed into the product rather than relying on inspection only.
3. Quality planning consists of identifying the standards for the project.
4. Metrics should be defined in order to objectively define the standards and allowable tolerance.
5. The approach to ensuring project quality should be documented in a Quality Management Plan.

Key Terminology

Metric: A numerical value used to make objective quality measurements.

Quality: A product's fitness for its purpose, defined as having the right features and being delivered with few errors.

Quality Management Plan: A planning document that describes the quality standards to be achieved for the project.

Standard: A level or grade that may be used as a measure of quality.

Tolerance: The maximum allowable variance from the standard or specifications of a project.

DISCUSSION QUESTIONS

1. Scope and quality are both related to the output of the project. What is the difference between these two concepts?
2. What are some of the ways that a Project Manager can encourage project team members to continuously improve the processes of the project?
3. Think of a project from your personal, work, or school activities in which the quality of the results was not as you anticipated. What were the causes of the lower quality output?

4.   Perform an online search to research quality pioneers. Choose a quality pioneer who is not cited in this chapter and describe this person's approach to quality.

NOTES

1.   Juran, J. M., & De Feo, J. A. (2010). *Juran's Quality Handbook: The Complete Guide to Performance Excellence*, p. 5. McGraw-Hill, New York, NY.
2.   Deming, W. E. (2000). *Out of the Crisis*, p. 29. The MIT Press, Cambridge, MA.

Risk Planning

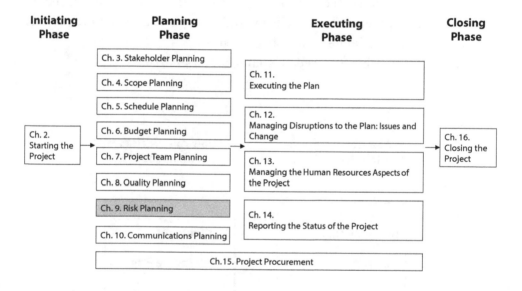

Initiating Phase	Planning Phase	Executing Phase	Closing Phase

Ch. 2. Starting the Project

Ch. 3. Stakeholder Planning
Ch. 4. Scope Planning
Ch. 5. Schedule Planning
Ch. 6. Budget Planning
Ch. 7. Project Team Planning
Ch. 8. Quality Planning
Ch. 9. Risk Planning
Ch. 10. Communications Planning

Ch. 11. Executing the Plan

Ch. 12. Managing Disruptions to the Plan: Issues and Change

Ch. 13. Managing the Human Resources Aspects of the Project

Ch. 14. Reporting the Status of the Project

Ch. 15. Project Procurement

Ch. 16. Closing the Project

INTRODUCTION TO RISK PLANNING

Too often overlooked, the management of **risk** is an essential component of successful project management. The complexity of a project environment provides many opportunities for things to go wrong. The limited amount of time available for the project puts pressure on the project team and may lead to problems. Given this environment, it is important to take a systematic approach to the management of risk.

One of the challenges of measuring the success of risk management is that when a potential problem is averted, nothing visible occurs. It is difficult to determine whether the problem was averted due to effective risk management or if it would have been avoided regardless.

For example, imagine that a plane is rerouted from its normal flight path because the air traffic controller spots a large flock of birds. When the potential crisis is averted, there is no way to be one hundred percent sure that the change in flight path prevented a bird from entering the plane's engine, as the birds may have ended up flying away even if the plane's flight path did not change. However, the air traffic controller's decisiveness represents diligent risk management given the information known at the time and the potential negative impact that could have occurred if no action was taken.

That being said, the benefits of project risk management should become apparent over time. Projects that exercise sound risk management practices should be observed to experience fewer problems and setbacks as compared to projects that ignore or practice limited risk management.

There are two main steps when planning for project risk:

Risk Planning

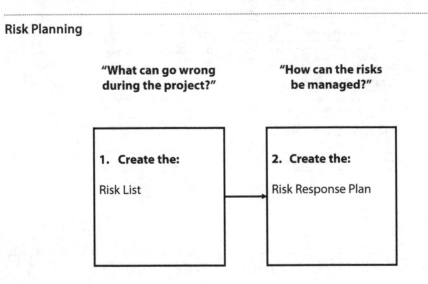

WHAT CAN GO WRONG DURING THE PROJECT?

The first step is to consider everything that could possibly go wrong during the project. An idea should not be ignored because "it will never happen." Often, the risk that was least expected ends up causing problems.

Team members and other stakeholders should be involved in the discussion, as they may be aware of additional risks. The scope of the project should be considered in order to identify potential problems. The documentation from previous projects may also be reviewed for additional ideas.

This work will result in a list of risks for the project. However, not all risks pose an equal threat. While some risks may cause severe problems if they occur, others may be minor issues only. Each identified risk should be assessed in order to determine its severity level. This allows the risks to be put in order from the highest level of severity to the lowest.

When assessing risk, there are two factors that should be estimated:
- The probability that the risk will occur
- The impact to the project if the risk does occur

Determining the probability of a risk is challenging as it is difficult to predict the future with complete accuracy. However, through judgment and experience, a reasonable estimate is usually possible. A qualitative method may be used to express the probability (e.g., high, medium, and low) or a quantitative method (e.g., 10%, 20%).

The second factor is to assess the impact to the project if the risk does occur. Possible impacts include:
- project delays;
- higher costs;
- dissatisfied project stakeholders;
- lower quality.

Determining the impact of a risk is also challenging, as there are many variables that affect what happens during a project. Again, through judgment and experience, a reasonable estimate of the impact is usually possible. A qualitative method may be used to express the impact (e.g., high, medium, and low) or a quantitative method (e.g., the financial cost to the project).

There are various factors to consider when determining whether to use a qualitative or quantitative method. Quantitative methods are more precise, allowing for an effective comparison of risks. For example, a risk that is estimated to have a probability of 50% is more severe than a risk that is estimated at 40%. However, team members are not always comfortable estimating quantitative probabilities and impacts.

Since qualitative methods are more general, team members tend to be more comfortable assigning assessments such as medium or low. The downside of this approach is that it is less precise. For example, if two risks are estimated to have a medium probability and a medium impact, it is difficult to determine which one is more severe.

K. Heldman (2005) created an approach that incorporates both qualitative and quantitative aspects.[1] Using this method, the probability of each identified risk will be assessed according to the table below.

Probability Table

PROBABILITY	PROBABILITY FACTOR	DESCRIPTION
Very Likely	.8	Occurs frequently during projects. Conditions are present for its occurrence during the project.
Likely	.5	Occurs sometimes during projects. Some conditions are present for its occurrence during the project.
Unlikely	.2	Does not generally occur during projects. Conditions are not present for its occurrence during the project.

Using this method, the probability of each identified risk will be assessed with a probability factor of .8, .5, or .2. Note that the probability factor does not equate to the probability of the risk occurring. For example, the very likely category does not indicate that there is an 80% chance that the risk will occur. Instead, using this system, a risk assessed as very likely is considered to be four times more likely to occur than a risk assessed as unlikely.

The impact of each identified risk will be assessed according to the following table, in which the result will have an impact factor of 10, 8, 5, or 2:

Impact Table

IMPACT	IMPACT FACTOR	DESCRIPTION
Critical	10	The occurrence of the risk would be catastrophic for the project with significant impact to the organization's finances, performance, or reputation.
Severe	8	The occurrence of the risk would be severe for the project with a high impact to the organization's finances, performance, or reputation.
Moderate	5	The occurrence of the risk would be a moderate issue for the project but is unlikely to significantly impact the organization's finances, performance, or reputation.
Low	2	The occurrence of the risk would be negligible for the project and would not impact the organization's finances, performance, or reputation.

Based on an assessment of the probability and impact, a risk score can be calculated by multiplying the probability factor by the impact factor. This creates a range of risk scores from .04 (unlikely probability and low impact) to 8 (very likely probability and critical impact). Now the list of risks may be sorted into priority order from the highest risk score to the lowest. The assessed risks may then be placed into the following **Risk List** template:

Risk List Template

RISK LIST					
Project Name					
[This section contains the project name that should appear consistently on all project documents. Organizations often have project naming conventions.]					
#	**Risk**	**Description**	**Prob Factor**	**Impact Factor**	**Risk Score**
[1, 2, etc.]	[Name of the risk.]	[Full description of the risk.]	Very likely (.8) Likely (.5) Unlikely (.2)	Critical (10) High (8) Med (5) Low (2)	[Prob factor multiplied by impact factor.]

Case Study Update: Creating the Risk List

Sophie's gathered her project team together to plan for possible risks. She calls the meeting to order.

"I've called the meeting today so that we, as a team, can plan for what could go wrong during the DecoCam V4 Product Launch project. We've had a lot of problems on other projects recently. I think if we put some additional focus on risk management, we can reduce the number of problems for this project."

Jason, the team's Business Analyst, leans forward in his chair. "I hear you, Sophie, but many things that have happened in the past were outside of our control. What could we do about it anyways?"

"Fair enough, Jason," Sophie replies. "But even for these issues, it would be useful for us to have a backup plan. And I bet there are many potential problems that are well within our control—we want to prevent them from ever happening."

Sophie then hands out a few blank cards to each team member. She asks each person to write down as many potential problems as they can. While the team may be tempted

Continued

to eliminate ideas, it is best to allow for an open flow of ideas and not filter anything at this point.

Within a few minutes, a number of completed cards are scattered across the table. Sophie writes each risk on the whiteboard:

1. Team member leaves the project.
2. Written materials contain errors.
3. Product launch is moved to an earlier date.
4. New requirements are received.
5. Trade show material costs are higher than expected.
6. Delivery of trade show materials is delayed.
7. The promotional video is late.
8. Promotional video's language translations are incorrect.
9. Social media posts attract inappropriate replies.
10. Multimedia demo causes disorientation to customers.

Sophie and the project team proceed to discuss and plan for each risk in detail. This includes creating a longer description of each risk, as well as selecting the probability factor and impact factor of each risk. Then, they calculate the risk score for each risk and put them in order from the highest score to the lowest.

The following is the Risk List that was created for the case study project:

Risk List

RISK LIST					
Project Name					
DCV4Launch–DecoCam V4 Product Launch					
#	**Risk**	**Description**	**Prob Factor**	**Impact Factor**	**Risk Score**
8	Promotional video's language transla-tions are incorrect.	Incorrect translation of the video to French and Spanish results in customer complaints and negative publicity.	.8	8	6.4
2	Written materials contain errors.	Errors are found in the written materi-als such as the press release, website updates, etc.	.5	10	5.0

6	Delivery of trade show materials is delayed.	Delivery of trade show materials is delayed.	.8	5	4.0
1	Team member leaves the project.	A team member leaves the project for a prolonged period of time for any reason, such as leaving the company or illness.	.5	5	2.5
9	Social media posts attract inappropriate replies.	The social media posts created for the product launch attract inappropriate replies that result in negative publicity.	.5	5	2.5
3	Product launch is moved to an earlier date.	The release date of DecoCam V4 is moved up, necessitating an earlier product launch date.	.2	10	2.0
7	The promotional video is late.	The promotional video takes longer than expected and is not available for the product launch.	.2	8	1.6
4	New requirements are received.	New requirements are received after planning is complete, causing changes to the project's deliverables.	.5	2	1.0
10	Multimedia demo causes disorientation to customers.	The multimedia demo's virtual reality causes disorientation and dizziness to some customers.	.2	5	1.0
5	Trade show material costs are higher than expected.	When ordering the tradeshow materials (e.g., the banner stand), the actual costs are higher than originally budgeted.	.2	2	0.4

HOW CAN THE RISKS BE MANAGED?

The list of risks identified in the previous section could cause significant problems to the project if one or many of them occur. It is clear that the project would be much more successful if the risks are avoided. Rather than leave this to chance, the Project Manager should make a risk response plan to manage the identified risks before they occur.

There are four types of risk response plans:

- **Risk acceptance:** the possibility that the risk will occur is accepted and therefore no action is taken until the risk occurs.
- **Risk mitigation:** actions are defined that reduce the probability or impact of the risk.
- **Risk avoidance:** the conditions that cause the risk are removed from the project scope, eliminating any possibility of the risk.

- **Risk transfer:** the impact of the risk is transferred to another entity outside of the project. The most common examples are transferring the risk to an individual (e.g., a waiver) or an organization (e.g., purchasing insurance).

Note that if risk management processes are not performed, all risks will default to the risk acceptance response type.

For each of the risk response types other than avoidance, a portion of the original probability and impact may still remain. This is known as residual risk. The following describes the residual risk for each of the risk response types:

- Risk acceptance: since no actions are taken, the residual risk will be equal to the original identified risk.
- Risk mitigation: the residual risk will be equal to the reduced probability and impact that remain once the defined actions are performed.
- Risk avoidance: the residual risk will be zero given that the scope was changed to eliminate the risk.
- Risk transfer: the residual risk will be equal to any remaining probability and impact that remain after the risk transfer. For example, if insurance is purchased, a deductible may need to be paid if the risk occurs.

Given the presence of residual risk, some risks will occur during a project. The final step of risk response planning is to determine the actions to perform if a risk occurs. These actions are referred to as **contingency plans**.

Those new to risk management may question why contingency plans are needed. Couldn't they just be planned if and when the risk occurs? Why spend all this effort for something that may not happen?

Reasons for contingency planning include:

1. Determining the best course of action when problems are occurring, and perhaps even in a crisis situation, is difficult. Considering the risk in advance without the pressure of the problem allows for a more measured plan.
2. A contingency plan helps identify processes that should be created in advance and would be too late to do so once the problem occurs. For example, bringing a first aid kit to a project involving a physical activity would be very helpful in case of injury.

The following is the template for the **Risk Response Plan**:

Risk Response Plan Template

RISK RESPONSE PLAN				
Project Name				
[This section contains the project name that should appear consistently on all project documents. Organizations often have project naming conventions.]				
#	**Risk**	**Risk Response**	**Description**	**Contingency Plan**
[1, 2, etc.]	[Name of the risk.]	[Accept/ Mitigate/ Avoid/ Transfer]	[Detailed description of how the selected risk response type will be implemented. Not required if the accept response type is selected.]	[Detailed description of the contingency plan. Includes the conditions that would cause the contingency plan to be invoked.]

An Example of Risk Response Planning

The four risk response types are often confused with each other. Before proceeding to the case study project, the following example will be explored in order to differentiate each of the four types.

Consider that you just purchased a new phone and you're concerned that you may lose it. For this example, the likelihood of this occurrence is assessed to be unlikely, while the impact would be severe.

There are four possible risk response strategies available to you:

- Accept the risk: if you happen to lose it, you will deal with it at that point.
- Mitigate the risk: develop careful procedures when using your phone, such as always keeping the phone in the same location and making a point to always check that the phone is in this location before traveling. You could also download a "phone finder" application to help recover your phone if it gets lost.
- Avoid the risk: you can choose not to own a phone.
- Transfer the risk: you could purchase phone replacement insurance from your service provider.

Notice that each risk response strategy has advantages and disadvantages. Acceptance takes the least effort but does not reduce the probability or impact of the risk. Mitigation reduces the severity of the risk but takes additional effort and the risk may still occur. Avoidance completely eliminates the risk but it is the most restrictive option. Transference often requires an ongoing cost (in this example, an insurance premium would be paid).

Case Study Update: Create the Risk Response Plan

Sophie looks at the list of risks and prepares to address the project team.

"I don't want any of these risks to occur during the project. So, is there anything we can do now to make them less of an issue later on?"

For the low priority risks, the team decides that no additional actions are needed. For other risks, they make a list of additional actions that they could perform that will help lessen the seriousness of the risks. For one risk in particular—the translation of the promotional video to other languages—they decide that the risk of problems is too high and they recommend that the requirement be removed from the project's scope.

Next, the team considers each risk and considers what actions should be taken if the risk occurs and what would trigger these actions during the project.

Sophie records the minutes of the meeting, ensuring that the activities discussed are accurately documented.

The following is the Risk Response Plan that was created for the case study project:

Risk Response Plan

RISK RESPONSE PLAN				
Project Name				
DCV4Launch–DecoCam V4 Product Launch				
#	**Risk**	**Risk Response**	**Description**	**Contingency Plan**
8	Promotional video's language translations are incorrect.	Avoid	This requirement should be re-moved from the project due to the negative publicity that may occur if errors are made. Further work to improve the organiza-tion's translation capabilities should be performed.	The risk is avoided. No contingency plan.

| 2 | Written materials contain errors. | Mitigate | Strict attention must be paid to the quality processes throughout the project. | Printed materials will be recalled and reproduced. The electronic material will be immediately corrected.

This plan is invoked when the error is reported. |
| 6 | Delivery of trade show materials is delayed. | Mitigate | Schedule trade show materials to be delivered at least one week before they are required. | Negotiate earlier delivery date with suppliers. Inform the trade show team of the possible delay.

This plan is invoked when materials are more than two days late from their original delivery date. |
| 1 | Team member leaves the project. | Mitigate | Ensure all project documentation and files are saved in the shared folder. Ensure all team members provide weekly progress updates. | Reassign work to other team members. Work with the Resource Manager to replace the missing team member as soon as possible.

This plan is invoked when:
1. Team member is absent for more than three consecutive days.
2. Team member resigns. |
| 9 | Social media posts attract inappropriate replies. | Accept | This risk is accepted as the team cannot control the replies to social media posts. | Remove any offensive posts according to the company's social media policy.

This plan is invoked when the inappropriate reply is detected. Replies to social media posts should be monitored at least twice per day. |
| 10 | Multimedia demo causes disorientation to customers. | Transfer | Create signs indicating that the demo may cause disorientation or dizziness and that people should use the demo at their own risk.
Mitigate by ensuring that people must be seated when viewing the demo. | Stop the multimedia demo and provide assistance as necessary.

This plan is invoked if a trade show participant displays signs of disorientation or dizziness. |

Continued

3	Product launch is moved to an earlier date.	Mitigate	Activities will be scheduled to be completed as soon as possible.	Add another videographer from another area of the company. The Business Analyst will assist the other team members with their activities. This plan is invoked if the product launch date is moved.
7	The promotional video is late.	Mitigate	Weekly checkpoints are planned in order to review the progress of the video.	Add another videographer from another area of the company. This plan is invoked if the video falls behind schedule by five days or more.
4	New requirements are received.	Accept	This risk is accepted as the project scope has been planned effectively and additional requirements gathering is not recommended.	Requested changes will be assessed and either approved or rejected according to the project's change management process. This plan is invoked when a new requirement is requested.
5	Trade show material costs are higher than expected.	Accept	This risk is accepted as the trade show material costs are a small percentage of the overall project budget.	Investigate alternate suppliers if available. Otherwise, the budget will be adjusted for the higher cost. This plan is invoked when the trade show material costs are 10% or more over budget.

CHAPTER SUMMARY

Key Concepts

1. Everything that could go wrong during the project is documented in the Risk List.
2. An assessment of the probability and impact of each risk is documented in the Risk List.
3. The actions to be taken before the risk occurs are documented in the Risk Response Plan.
4. The actions to be taken if the risk does occur are documented in the Risk Response Plan.

Key Terminology

Contingency Plan: The actions to be performed in the event that the defined risks occur.

Risk: A potential situation that could cause a negative impact to the project.

Risk Acceptance: The possibility that the risk will occur is accepted and therefore no action is taken until the risk occurs.

Risk Avoidance: The conditions that cause the risk are removed from the project scope, eliminating any possibility of the risk.

Risk List: A planning document that contains all identified risks for the project and includes their probability factor, impact factor, and risk score.

Risk Mitigation: Actions are defined that reduce the probability or impact of the risk.

Risk Response Plan: A planning document that indicates the risk response(s) and contingency plan for each identified risk.

Risk Transfer: The impact of the risk is transferred to another entity outside of the project.

DISCUSSION QUESTIONS

1. Risk response plans and contingency plans are often misunderstood. What is the difference between these two risk management concepts?
2. What is the difference between the risk avoidance and risk mitigation response strategies?
3. Think of a project from your personal, work, or school activities in which problems occurred during the project. Could these risks have been identified earlier in the project? Could the risk response plans discussed in this chapter (i.e., accept, mitigate, avoid, and transfer) have been used?
4. Perform an online search to research common project management risks. Summarize five common risks and their possible risk response plans.

NOTE

1. Heldman, K. (2005). *Project Manager's Spotlight on Risk Management*. Jossey-Bass, San Francisco, CA.

10 Communications Planning

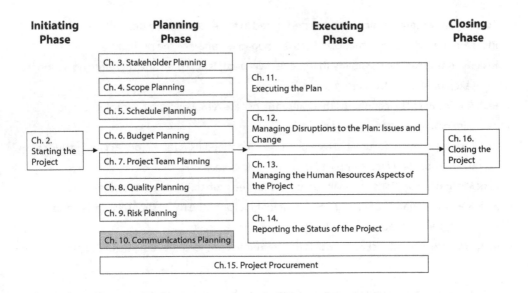

Initiating Phase	Planning Phase	Executing Phase	Closing Phase
	Ch. 3. Stakeholder Planning		
	Ch. 4. Scope Planning	Ch. 11. Executing the Plan	
	Ch. 5. Schedule Planning		
Ch. 2. Starting the Project	Ch. 6. Budget Planning	Ch. 12. Managing Disruptions to the Plan: Issues and Change	Ch. 16. Closing the Project
	Ch. 7. Project Team Planning	Ch. 13. Managing the Human Resources Aspects of the Project	
	Ch. 8. Quality Planning		
	Ch. 9. Risk Planning	Ch. 14. Reporting the Status of the Project	
	Ch. 10. Communications Planning		
	Ch.15. Project Procurement		

INTRODUCTION TO COMMUNICATIONS PLANNING

In order for a project to be successful, people need to work together to achieve the project's objectives. This requires the exchange of relevant information between people inside and outside the project at the appropriate time. To do this effectively, communications planning and coordination are required.

Project teams will often decide to communicate "when required" instead of developing a communication plan. This usually means that there is less communication between team members on a project, which can lead to an increased number of problems. More time is then spent on solving the problems and less time is spent on the communications that were to be performed "when required." This becomes a vicious cycle that leads to underperformance.

Unfortunately, planning communications may have negative connotations for those who see it as resulting in long, needless meetings and increased bureaucracy. Therefore, the challenge for the Project Manager is to develop a clear and practical communication plan. Regardless of whether a planned communication is a meeting, report, presentation, or email, care should be taken that each plan is necessary and adds to the performance of the project.

There are two main steps when planning for project communications:

Communications Planning

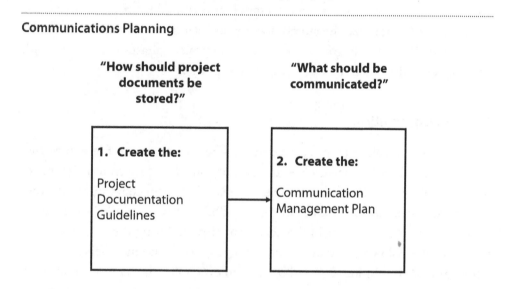

HOW SHOULD PROJECT DOCUMENTS BE STORED?

Project documentation consists of design documents, schedules, budgets, quality plans, risk information, status reports, issues, meeting agendas and minutes, presentations, and many other documents. The creation of documentation guidelines will make it easier to find and update these documents throughout the project. They will also help ensure that the documentation is kept current and that the project team is viewing and updating the latest version of each document.

The guidelines should address the following:
- Where will the documents be stored?
- How will the documents be organized?
- What is the naming convention for documents?
- What documents require multiple versions?

In some instances, the project's organization may already have established communication guidelines for projects.

Storage Location and Organization

The storage location for both electronic and hard copy project documents should be determined. Consider factors such as whether the documents will be backed up and if a secure passcode is required for all or certain documents.

In order to organize the stored documents, categories or folders should be considered. Possible categories/folders include project phases (e.g., Planning), and project or document types (e.g., Status Reports).

Naming Conventions

When saving documents, project team members often create file names that are meaningful only to themselves and do not consider other team members or projects. For example, if a team member creates a document containing the Work Breakdown Structure and names the file "WBS," how will this file be differentiated from the other versions of the document created during the project or from the Work Breakdown Structures from other projects? Team members should use a file naming convention that will be clear to everyone. The naming convention may include information such as the project name or code, the document name, the version (if applicable), and the date.

Since files are usually sorted in alphanumeric order, the structure of the naming convention should be created with this in mind.

Document Versions

For certain documents, multiple versions may be required in order to view the history of major updates to each document.

In these instances, a separate copy of each version is stored, with the latest version representing the current state of the document. The majority of project documents do not typically require separate versions.

The template for the **Project Documentation Guidelines** document is as follows:

Project Documentation Guidelines Template

PROJECT DOCUMENTATION GUIDELINES	
Project Name	[This section contains the project name that should appear consistently on all project documents. Organizations often have project naming conventions.]
Storage Location and Organization	
[This section describes the location of project documents and how they are organized.]	
Naming Conventions	
[This section describes the naming conventions for all project files.]	
Document Versions	
[This section indicates which documents require multiple versions.]	

Case Study Update: Creating the Project Documentation Guidelines

Sophie knows from past experience that effective communication is vital for her project. More often than not, whenever one of her projects has underperformed, the root cause was a problem with the way people communicated with each other.

During her last project, it was difficult for her project team to find the latest project documents. A great deal of time and effort was spent figuring out where documents were stored and, in some cases, mistakes were made because an incorrect document was used. This time, Sophie plans to set out the guidelines at the start of the project.

Sophie plans to store all documents on the project website using a new document management system recently purchased by Deco Productions. Folders will be set up to logically organize the documents and the company standard for project file names will be used. Lastly, Sophie will designate the documents that will require versions to be maintained.

What follows is the Project Documentation Guidelines for the case study project:

Project Documentation Guidelines

PROJECT DOCUMENTATION GUIDELINES	
Project Name	DCV4Launch–DecoCam V4 Product Launch

Storage Location and Organization

All project documents will be stored on the secured project website. Sophie Featherstone will be the administrator and will grant Read or Read/Write access to the project team and certain project stakeholders as needed.

Documents will be filed in the following folders:
- Initiating
- Scope
- Schedule
- Budget
- Team/HR
- Quality
- Risk
- Communication
- Meeting Agenda and Minutes
- Status Reports
- Issues
- Changes
- Closing

Naming Conventions

All document file names will be as follows:
Project ID - Document Name - Version (if required) - Date of Report (YYYYMMDD)

Examples:
- DCV4Launch - Project Charter - 1.0 - 20200325
- DCV4Launch - Project Status Report - 20200424

Document Versions

Document versions will be maintained for the Project Charter and Project Scope Statement. For all other project documents, only the latest version will be saved.

Major changes to the document will result in a new version number (e.g., 2.0, 3.0). Minor changes will result in a new decimal (e.g., 2.1, 2.2).

WHAT SHOULD BE COMMUNICATED?

It can be challenging to determine the content of a formal communication plan. It is not intended to document all of the informal communications that naturally take place during a project. Not only would this be a large and time-consuming task, but it would also be impractical to plan for this level of detail.

Instead, the content of a communication plan should contain details regarding the following communications that are planned to take place during the project:

- Communication of project information: this includes meetings, reports, emails, and information posted online. Communications of this type include the distribution of information, the collection of requirements, and the resolution of issues.
- Communication of project status information: this often includes a number of reports and meetings.

The communications are then documented in a **Communication Management Plan**. When creating this plan, the information needs of the project stakeholders should be considered. The goal should be to ensure that each stakeholder has access to the information they need to perform their role effectively. The Stakeholder Management Plan should also be consulted and any planned communications included in this document should be considered for possible inclusion in the Communication Management Plan.

The template for the Communication Management Plan is as follows:

Communication Management Plan Template

COMMUNICATION MANAGEMENT PLAN			
Project Name	[This section contains the project name that should appear consistently on all project documents. Organizations often have project naming conventions.]		
Communication Name	**Description**	**Audience**	**Timing**
[Short name of the communication.]	[Full description of the communication including the purpose and the communication medium to be used.]	[People or group to receive or attend to the communication.]	[Date or frequency of the communication.]

Case Study Update: Creating the Communication Management Plan

Sophie begins to think about the communications that should occur during the project. How much communication is needed? It would be nice to have frequent meetings, but when would the work itself get done? Should there be more face-to-face interaction or more information posted online? How often should the information be produced? All these questions pass through Sophie's mind as she considers how to plan the communications.

She then asks herself: "Who is it that the project needs to communicate with?" The answer is clear: the project stakeholders. With this insight, she pulls out the Stakeholder Analysis document and lists each stakeholder on a blank sheet of paper. She considers the different reasons that she might have to communicate with them, such as a status update or a review of daily work tasks. She then proceeds to list the reasons under each stakeholder name.

Sophie considers different communication mediums, such as meetings, phone calls, emails, or written reports, and asks herself which one would be the most effective for each of the requirements on her list. Next, she considers the timing. If it is a one-time communication, when should it occur? If it is a recurring communication, how often should it occur?

As Sophie finishes this process, she reviews the results of her work: a document outlining the various communications that will be performed during the project. While she knows that effective communication will be an ongoing challenge, she's feeling a lot more confident now that she has a plan.

The following is the Communication Management Plan for the case study project:

Communication Management Plan

COMMUNICATION MANAGEMENT PLAN			
Project Name	DCV4Launch–DecoCam V4 Product Launch		
Communication Name	**Description**	**Audience/ Attendees**	**Timing**
Project Kickoff Meeting	Meeting to review the Project Charter for the project and obtain formal approval to proceed to the Planning Phase.	Casey Serrador Arun Singh Sophie Featherstone	Mar 25, 2020
Distribution of the Project Charter	Project Charter sent as email by Sophie Featherstone.	Project Managers of the other V4 projects	Mar 27, 2020
Scope Review and Sign Off Meeting	Meeting to formally review the project plans and obtain approval to proceed to the Executing Phase.	Casey Serrador Arun Singh Project team	Apr 3, 2020

Daily Project Team Huddle	Daily 15-minute meeting of the product launch team to review the current status of the project and outstanding issues.	Project team	Daily, beginning: Apr 6, 2020
Project Status Report	Weekly status report. Email sent by Sophie Featherstone.	Arun Singh Project Managers of the other V4 projects	Weekly: Thursdays by noon
Project Status Review Meeting	Weekly review of all DecoCam V4 projects.	Arun Singh Project Managers of the other V4 projects	Weekly: Fridays at 1:00 p.m.
Company Announcement	An announcement of the new product launch. This information will be included in the Weekly Message Board.	Deco Productions employees	May 8, 2020
Lessons Learned	Meeting to review the lessons of the project in order to improve future projects.	Arun Singh Project team Adrian Binkley	May 11, 2020
Final Project Meeting	Final review of the project's results.	Casey Serrador Arun Singh Project team	May 13, 2020

CHAPTER SUMMARY

Key Concepts

1. The Project Documentation Guidelines should be created.
2. A Communications Management Plan containing the planned communications for the project should be created.

Key Terminology

Communication Management Plan: A planning document that contains all the planned communications for a project. The plan includes the name, description, intended audience, and the date or frequency of the communications.

Project Documentation Guidelines: A planning document that contains guidelines for the documentation of a project. The guidelines describe the storage location, preferred organization method, and the naming conventions for project files, and indicate which documents require multiple versions.

DISCUSSION QUESTIONS

1. Describe the possible problems that may occur during a project if communications are not planned in advance.

2. In the case study example, the press release and outreach activities were included in the project schedule, but not in the Communication Management Plan. Should these activities also have been included in the Communication Management Plan?

3. Think of a project from your personal, work, or school activities in which problems occurred during the project. Could any of these problems have been averted or reduced through more effective communication?

4. Perform an online search to research project communication best practices. Summarize your findings.

PART III

THE EXECUTING PHASE

With the completion of the Planning Phase, the project plans are complete and the project is ready to move to the Executing Phase. The plans may be reviewed with the Project Sponsor and other stakeholders to gain approval to proceed with the completion of the project. The purpose of the Executing Phase is to produce the deliverables of the project by carrying out the project plans.

The creation of the project's product, service, or result takes place during this phase. The project team increases in size with the team members added to the project as planned in the HR Requirements document.

There is also a change in atmosphere as the project moves from planning to executing. Whereas planning usually involves a small number of people creating written plans and documents, executing involves a larger number of people creating the actual deliverables. It is the action-oriented time of the project that includes the completion of the work, the management of the team, the resolution of issues, and ongoing communication with the project stakeholders.

11 Executing the Plan

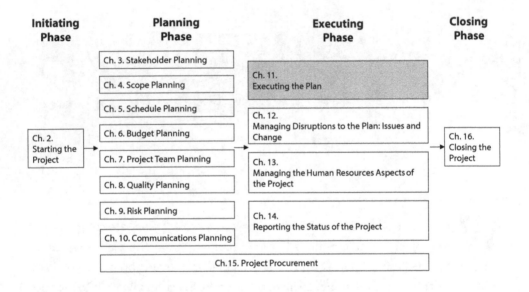

INTRODUCTION TO EXECUTING THE PLAN

After the Planning Phase, the next step is to execute the plan in order to create the deliverables of the project. This involves the following:

- Performing the activities of the schedule
- Producing the scope
- Maintaining the budget
- Monitoring the risks
- Creating the communications
- Managing the quality of the deliverables

PERFORMING THE ACTIVITIES OF THE SCHEDULE

The actions taken during execution should follow the project schedule to ensure that all activities are completed. For example, the portion of the case study project schedule related to the Trade Show Signage is shown below:

Project Schedule (Trade Show Signage)

DecoCam V4 Prod Launch	Dur	27-Mar M T W T F	3-Apr M T W T F	10-Apr M T W T F
Initiating				
Initiate the project	3d			
Project approved	0d			
Planning				
Plan the project	7d			
Executing				
Trade show signage				
Create sign graphics/text	3d			
Order banner stands	1d			

The project schedule tends to be the most dynamic of all the project planning documents. The timing and duration of activities will often vary from the original plan for a variety of reasons, including:

- the work takes longer than expected;
- the person working on the activity is unavailable or has reduced availability;
- the scope of the project has increased;
- external factors that were not predicted.

If the project begins to fall behind schedule, there are a number of approaches to shorten the duration of a project.

Process Improvement

When a reduced amount of time is available, this can motivate the project team to devise innovative approaches that result in less time and effort being spent to complete the required work. While there are limits to this approach, there are often efficiencies that may be gained through process improvement.

Overlapping Activities

During the original planning, tasks are often planned to be sequential, as this is the simplest approach to completing the work. If the project begins to fall behind schedule, the timing of activities may be changed to increase the level of overlap. Activities may be scheduled to overlap slightly (i.e., by a few days or a short amount of time) or completely (i.e., scheduled to occur at the same time).

Increasing the overlap of activities tends to increase the cost of the project. Because an increasing amount of work is done in parallel rather than sequentially, increased communication and coordination are required to complete the work. There is also the potential for more rework, as changes made in an activity may affect work already completed in another activity. The increased complexity of overlapping activities may also negatively affect the quality of the project.

Adding More Resources to Activities

Another approach is to add more resources to activities in order to complete them earlier. This can take the form of additional human resources or by increasing the work hours of the people already assigned to the activities.

As with overlapping activities, adding resources will usually increase the cost of the project. While the activities will be completed sooner, the increased communication, coordination, and potential for rework (due to increased numbers of workers and longer hours) will likely increase the cost of the project. The quality may also suffer as the increased number of workers often leads to an increased likelihood of miscommunications and other errors.

Reducing the Scope of the Project

Eliminating scope from the project can also cause the project to be completed earlier. This would be a significant change to the project and would likely require the approval of the Project Sponsor.

Other than development process improvements, each of the methods listed above involves trade-offs that the Project Manager would need to carefully consider. In each case, the impact to the project's cost, scope, and quality would be balanced against the shortened project schedule.

PRODUCING THE SCOPE

The Project Scope Statement and supporting documents provide a description of the deliverables to be produced during the project. For example, during the case study project, the Trade Show Signage work package was described as follows:

Project Scope Statement (Trade Show Signage)

PROJECT SCOPE STATEMENT	
Project Name	DCV4Launch–DecoCam V4 Product Launch
Project Deliverables	
Trade Show Support	Trade Show Signage • The signs will be retractable banner stands. • Initial creation of five stands. • Integrate with company's existing trade show set up and branding. • Provide a visual display of the product's features. • Display information with links to more product information. • Update the trade show supplies procedures and data files to allow for the order of additional banners.

During execution, the project team should execute the Trade Show Signage exactly as described above. After creating each deliverable contained in the Project Scope Statement, the full scope of the project will be completed.

MONITORING THE BUDGET

The costs that were previously estimated during planning will be incurred during the Executing Phase. In some cases, the costs may be equal to what was planned, but usually there will be either a positive or negative variance. For example, the team members may take more or less time than estimated to complete the activities. Additionally, the cost of the required materials may work out to be more or less than the estimate. Unexpected problems will usually increase costs, while unforeseen opportunities may lower costs.

All expenditures should be managed carefully during the project. For example, the cost of each camera and tripod was estimated to be $700. If the cost quoted by a supplier turns out to be $1,500, further action may be required.

In addition to managing costs as they occur, costs incurred should be tracked and compared to the budget. The following demonstrates the Detailed Budget of the case study at the end of the third week.

Detailed Budget After Three Weeks

DETAILED BUDGET									
Project Name	DCV4Launch–DecoCam V4 Product Launch								
Cost Category	**Week ending 27-Mar**	**Week ending 3-Apr**	**Week ending 10-Apr**	**Week ending 17-Apr**	**Week ending 24-Apr**	**Week ending 1-May**	**Week ending 8-May**	**Week ending 15-May**	**Total**
Initiating									
HR costs	$1,200								**$1,200**
Planning									
HR costs	$2,080	$5,200							**$7,280**
Executing									
HR costs			$8,800	$8,800	$10,400	$7,840	$6,400		**$42,240**
Other costs			$1,000	$2,000	$1,600				**$4,600**
Closing									
HR costs								$1,200	**$1,200**
Total Costs	**$3,280**	**$5,200**	**$9,800**	**$10,800**	**$12,000**	**$7,840**	**$6,400**	**$1,200**	**$56,520**
Actual Costs	**$4,200**	**$5,000**	**$9,900**						**$19,100**
Variance	**$920**	**($200)**	**$100**						**$820**

At the end of the third week, the plan was to have spent $18,280 ($3,280 + $5,200 + $9,800). However, the actual amount spent is $19,100 ($4,200 + $5,000 + $9,900). This means that project is $820 over budget after three weeks. If this trend was to continue, the team could exceed its overall budget for the project.

The Project Manager should review the costs to date in order to determine the likelihood that this trend will continue during the remainder of the project and if any actions should be taken.

MONITORING THE RISKS

As the project proceeds, conditions may change, which could either increase or decrease the level of risk.

The Risk Response Plan should be monitored during the execution of the project in order to:

- add new risks that become apparent;
- determine whether the risk response plans remain appropriate and are being performed as needed;
- determine whether the contingency plans remain appropriate and whether they should be put into action.

The following demonstrates the Risk Response Plan for the two risks related to the trade show materials.

Risk Response Plan (Trade Show)

RISK RESPONSE PLAN			
Project Name			
DCV4Launch–DecoCam V4 Product Launch			
#	**Risk**	**Risk Response**	**Description** ⁞ **Contingency Plan**

#	Risk	Risk Response	Description	Contingency Plan
6	Delivery of trade show materials is delayed.	Mitigate	Schedule trade show materials to be delivered at least one week before they are required.	Negotiate earlier delivery date with suppliers. Inform the trade show team of the possible delay. This plan is invoked when materials are more than two days late from their original delivery date.
5	Trade show material costs are higher than expected.	Accept	This risk is accepted as the trade show material costs are a small percentage of the overall project budget.	Investigate alternate suppliers if available. Otherwise, the budget will be adjusted for the higher cost. This plan is invoked when the trade show material costs are 10% or more over budget.

For Risk #6, the Project Manager ensures the delivery date is scheduled as planned. If the delivery were late by two days or more, the Project Manager would invoke the contingency plan.

For Risk #5, the Project Manager reviews the material costs. If they are higher than the budgeted amount, the contingency plan is put into action.

This constant level of attention will help ensure that the Risk Response Plan remains current and relevant.

CREATING THE COMMUNICATIONS

During the execution of the project, the Communication Management Plan should be periodically consulted to ensure that the planned communications are being carried out. These may be one-time communications (e.g., the company announcement on May 8th) or they may be recurring communications (e.g., the Project Status Report, every Thursday at noon).

The effectiveness of the project's communication should be continuously reviewed and assessed. This may result in adjustments to the Communication Management Plan to improve the level of communication.

Case Study Update: Executing the Plan

With the project now in full swing, Sophie settles into her task of ensuring that all the deliverables of the project are created as planned. The design of the trade show banners has just been completed and reviewed by the Marketing department. Based on their feedback, a few minor adjustments were made and the order was submitted on time.

The project has been proceeding on schedule so far, though one of her team members (Eli) was sick for a couple of days which caused some delays on his activities. Through a combination of adding some overtime hours and assigning Jason to one of Eli's activities, the project was put back on schedule.

Sophie notices that the costs are running higher than expected after the first three weeks. She will look into this immediately as she does not want the project to go over budget.

After opening the Risk Response Plan, she scans each risk. One of the highest risks is that the written material produced by the project contains spelling or grammatical errors. She notices that the plan is to mitigate the risk through strict attention to quality processes in this area. She makes a mental note to add this to tomorrow's project team meeting agenda.

She's also been steadily working through the Communication Management Plan by making sure all of the planned communications have been scheduled. All are in place so far except for the final two communications that will occur later in the project (i.e., the company announcement and the Final Project Meeting).

Overall, Sophie is feeling good about the progress of the project.

MANAGING THE QUALITY OF THE DELIVERABLES

During the Planning Phase, the relevant quality standards for the project were defined and recorded in the Quality Management Plan. During execution, the quality of the deliverables produced is managed in order to ensure that they meet these standards.

In order to manage the quality, there are two main functions: quality assurance and quality control. While they are presented as separate functions, during projects they are often performed by the same individuals or team members who may perform both functions repeatedly over a period a time.

Quality Assurance

The goal of quality assurance is to develop processes to prevent or detect project defects. These processes are documented in the **Quality Assurance Plan**.

The first part of this plan documents the quality processes that should be followed throughout the project. For example, a process could be established requiring all written material to be verified using the company's standard spelling and grammar checking software. The second part of the plan documents the specific tests that should be performed to verify the quality of each project deliverable.

The template for the Quality Assurance Plan is as follows:

Quality Assurance Plan Template

QUALITY ASSURANCE PLAN		
Project Name		
[This section contains the project name that should appear consistently on all project documents. Organizations often have project naming conventions.]		
Quality Assurance Processes		
[Include a list of all processes to be used during the project to ensure that the quality goals are achieved.]		
Test Plan		
Deliverable	**Test Cases**	**Performed By**
[Work package from the WBS.]	[A full description of the test(s) that should be performed to verify the quality of the work package.]	[The name of the person(s) who should perform the test(s).]

Case Study Update: Creating the Quality Assurance Plan

Sophie has a small sign propped on her desk with the popular adage: "Anything that can go wrong will go wrong." When she bought it at a novelty store a couple of years ago, she thought Murphy's Law was just a funny quote. Now, after a few projects, she knows that it tends to be all too true.

For this reason, she puts a great deal of focus on quality assurance during her projects. She's a great believer in creating effective processes that help to prevent problems from occurring. While Deco Productions has a standard list of quality assurance processes, she's always looking to enhance them for her project. For example, at the daily team huddle, a new process has been introduced: each team member provides informal demonstrations of their deliverables as they are developed. This leads to an increased awareness of all ongoing projects, which results in fewer defects resulting from communication problems and misunderstandings.

The Quality Assurance Plan for the case study project is as follows:

Quality Assurance Plan

QUALITY ASSURANCE PLAN
Project Name
DCV4Launch–DecoCam V4 Product Launch
Quality Assurance Processes

1. All written materials are verified with the company's standard spelling and grammar checking software.

2. All project deliverables are verified as follows:
   - Test #1: The team member who creates the deliverable will verify that it meets the defined specifications.
   - Test #2: Jason will perform the tests defined in the Test Plan below.

3. Each team member will provide an overview of their recently completed work at the daily team huddle.

Test Plan		
Deliverable	**Description**	**Performed By**
Trade Show Signage	Test #1	Chris
	Test #2: 1. Spelling/grammar of all text contains no errors. 2. Graphics according to company standards. 3. Information on the banner is accurate (e.g., names, links, dates). 4. Banner stand meets the size requirements.	Jason

Booth Giveaways	Test #1	Chris
	Test #2: 1. Spelling/grammar of all text contains no errors. 2. Graphics according to company standards. 3. Information on the giveaway is accurate (e.g., names, links, dates).	Jason
Multimedia Demo	Test #1	Chris
	Test #2: 1. Multimedia demo instructions contain no spelling/grammar errors. 2. Multimedia demo instructions accurately describe the demo. 3. Repeated use of the demo does not cause dizziness or other physical effects.	Jason
Social Media	Test #1	Sarah
	Test #2: 1. Spelling/grammar of all text contains no errors. 2. All names and titles are correct.	Jason
Website Updates	Test #1	Sarah
	Test #2: 1. Spelling/grammar of all text contains no errors. 2. All names and titles are correct.	Jason
Press Release	Test #1	Sarah
	Test #2: 1. Spelling/grammar of all text contains no errors. 2. Information in the press release is accurate (e.g., names, links, dates). 3. Meets CP style standards	Jason
Promotional Video	Test #1	Maddy
	Test #2: 1. Video is viewable on all major devices. 2. Spelling/grammar of all text contains no errors. 3. Information in the video is accurate (e.g., names, links, dates).	Jason

Quality Control

During **quality control**, the focus shifts to the product. The deliverables are verified according to the test plans defined in the Quality Assurance Plan.

As the deliverables are created, the quality control processes are performed. Records are maintained regarding the success or failure of each test. If there is a failure, the defect is communicated to the appropriate project team member(s) to be resolved. Once the correction is made, the quality control processes are repeated to test the updated deliverable. This cycle is repeated until no defects are found.

If any subsequent changes are made to the deliverable later on, then the quality control processes would need to be repeated to ensure that a defect was not introduced because of the change.

Case Study Update: Performing Quality Control

As the deliverables are completed and each team member verifies their own work, Jason gets involved to perform the tests defined in the Quality Assurance Plan.

Over the years, Jason has developed a keen eye for defects, particularly spelling errors. While the team's work in this area has been very good, they are always amazed at how he can quickly locate a misplaced letter or punctuation error.

Jason makes sure that he keeps detailed records of the tests performed on each deliverable and that he is aware of any changes that occur after he has verified a deliverable. Even the smallest change can affect the quality of a deliverable at any point in the project.

As each deliverable is verified, the team grows increasingly confident about the overall quality of their product.

CHAPTER SUMMARY

Key Concepts

1. Produce the deliverables of the project by: performing the activities of the schedule, producing the scope, maintaining the budget, monitoring the risks, creating the communications, and managing the quality of the deliverables.
2. Create a plan to verify the quality of the project deliverables and document this information in the Quality Assurance Plan.
3. Verify the quality of the project deliverables.

Key Terminology

Quality Assurance Plan: A document containing the processes that will be implemented to improve the level of project quality and a description of the tests that will be performed to verify the quality of the deliverables.

Quality Control: The activities performed to verify the quality of the project deliverables according to the Quality Assurance Plan.

DISCUSSION QUESTIONS

1. You are at the midpoint of a project and have used only 30% of your budget. Does this mean that you will be under budget at the end of the project?

2. Think of a project from your personal, work, or school activities in which the work started to fall behind schedule and was in danger of being late. What did you do to get the work back on schedule?

3. One of your team members comes to you with an idea for continuous improvement. His idea is that rather than have a second person test the quality of an output, it would be more efficient to just have everyone verify their own output. How would you respond to this idea?

4. Quality assurance and quality control are closely related concepts. Perform an online search to research "quality assurance vs. quality control." Summarize your findings.

12 Managing Disruptions to the Plan: Issues and Change

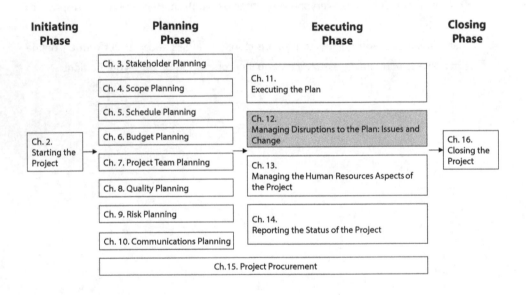

Initiating Phase	Planning Phase	Executing Phase	Closing Phase
	Ch. 3. Stakeholder Planning	Ch. 11. Executing the Plan	
	Ch. 4. Scope Planning		
	Ch. 5. Schedule Planning	Ch. 12. Managing Disruptions to the Plan: Issues and Change	
Ch. 2. Starting the Project	Ch. 6. Budget Planning		Ch. 16. Closing the Project
	Ch. 7. Project Team Planning	Ch. 13. Managing the Human Resources Aspects of the Project	
	Ch. 8. Quality Planning		
	Ch. 9. Risk Planning	Ch. 14. Reporting the Status of the Project	
	Ch. 10. Communications Planning		
	Ch. 15. Project Procurement		

INTRODUCTION TO MANAGING DISRUPTIONS TO THE PLAN

Ideally, the execution of the project would consist of systematically completing each aspect of the project plan. All aspects of the plan would have been planned thoroughly, all estimates would be accurate, no one would change their mind, and nothing in the business environment would change during the project. Unfortunately, this is not the reality of most projects. Instead, as projects are executed, they are constantly being bombarded by disruptions to the previously completed plan. These disruptions include:

- planning errors or omissions;
- project work taking longer than expected;
- new information becoming available to the project;
- project team performance problems;
- new or changing stakeholders;
- new or changing technology;
- changes in the business environment.

If they are not attended to, disruptions such as these will cause the project to underperform, as each disruption will cause the project to divert from its plan. As a result, the plan will become more difficult to manage successfully.

To prepare for this environment, it is vital to maintain sound processes to address project disruptions as they occur. There are two main processes: managing project issues and managing project change.

MANAGING PROJECT ISSUES

A project **issue** or problem is a condition or situation that, if left unresolved, will reduce the performance or effectiveness of the project. In order to successfully complete the project, it is important that the Project Manager documents, prioritizes, and resolves issues effectively.

Issues and risks are not the same. An issue is something that is presently occurring during the project. A risk is something that may occur in the future. If a risk does occur, it becomes an issue.

Documenting Issues

At any time, there are often many issues that are occurring for a project, especially for large or complex projects.

In order to manage the project effectively in this environment, a list of issues called an **Issue Log** is created. Not only does this provide a record of current issues, it also provides a history of issues previously resolved by the project team. Issue logs vary in terms of the information gathered for each issue, but as a minimum should contain: a description of the issue, its priority, its current status, and a unique identifier. The Issue Log template is as follows:

Issue Log Template

ISSUE LOG			
Project Name			
[This section contains the project name that should appear consistently on all project documents. Organizations often have project naming conventions.]			
Issue #	**Description**	**Priority**	**Status**
[1, 2, etc.]	[Full description of the issue with as much detail as needed or references to other documents. May include the name of the team member who has been assigned to resolve the issue. Once the issue is completed, this field should be updated to include the details of the resolution.]	[High/ Medium/ Low]	[Not started/ Started/ Completed/ NPW]

Assigning numbers to each issue is useful for instances when you may need to refer to a specific issue. For example, the project budget may have many related issues, and numbering the issues reduces the likelihood of confusing them.

Guidelines should be set for each priority value. For example, the high priority designation could be used for critical issues that must be resolved immediately. The medium designation could be used for very important issues to be addressed after all high priority issues are resolved. Low priority issues are relatively minor issues that could be addressed once all high and medium priority issues are resolved.

The status of the issue should be kept current. The normal progress of an issue would move from not started, to started, to completed. NPW stands for "not proceeded with" and should be used for issues that will not be addressed during the project.

Prioritizing Issues

It is useful to create the Issue Log using spreadsheet software that can filter and sort the issues according to their priority and/or status.

For example, the Project Manager could filter the spreadsheet to only show the not started issues and then sort them from high to low priority. This would clearly demonstrate the priority of issues that are not currently started.

Resolving Issues

In order to resolve issues, a problem-solving approach should be used. Depending on the size and complexity of an issue, this process may be performed formally involving written documentation and analysis (for large issues) or may be performed quickly and informally with minimal documentation (for small issues). The following steps describe the problem-solving process.

1. Fully Describe the Issue

In order to resolve the issue, it is important to fully describe the nature of the issue in as much detail as possible.

2. Develop Alternative Solutions

Depending on the nature of the issue, there are often many alternative solutions available. At this stage, it is important that different alternatives are considered and the team does not get locked into a single solution. For example, even in situations where an error occurs, at least two alternatives usually exist: correct the error or do nothing (i.e., live with the error).

Creative solutions should be considered at this point. Problems often cause the team to look at the project in different ways, which may help them to generate innovative solutions.

The costs and benefits of each alternative should be estimated. Some alternatives may solve the problem very effectively but may cause an increase in the project budget or a delay in the project schedule. Other alternatives may solve the problem but may increase the risk for the project.

3. Select the Optimal Solution

In some instances, choosing the most appropriate solution to resolve an issue is straightforward. In cases where the choice is less obvious, a number of approaches may be used to select the optimal solution, including the following:

- Comparison of the costs and benefits: for this method, the costs and benefits are compared. This approach tends to be useful when the costs and benefits are quantifiable and allow for an effective comparison.
- Weighted average: for this method, a set of criteria is developed for making the decision and a weight is assigned to each criteria. Then, a score is assigned for each potential solution based on those weightings.

The following example illustrates how to assign weighted scores to potential project solutions. In the example, there are three different criteria: the cost, timeliness, and effectiveness of the solution. The weights that are assigned are 20%, 30%, and 50% respectively. There are two alternatives that are ranked from 1 (poor) to 10 (best) for each of the criteria. The table below summarizes the results:

Weighted Scores

	COST (20%)		TIME (30%)		EFFECTIVE (50%)	
	Score	Weighted Score	Score	Weighted Score	Score	Weighted Score
Alternative 1	5	1.0	6	1.8	9	4.5
Alternative 2	8	1.6	6	1.8	5	2.5

The total weighted scores are:
- Alternative 1: 1.0 + 1.8 + 4.5 = 7.3
- Alternative 2: 1.6 + 1.8 + 2.5 = 5.9

Therefore, based on the weighted averages, Alternative 1 would be the optimal solution to the issue.

If the selected alternative is within the project's approved budget, timeline, and scope, then the process will move on to step 4. However, if the selected alternative represents an increase to the approved budget, a delay to the timeline, or a change to the project scope, then additional approval may be required.

4. Implement the Selected Alternative
Once an alternative is selected, the actions required to implement this alternative should be scheduled and performed.

During the resolution of issues, there are often multiple issues occurring simultaneously and there may be limited time to research different alternatives. Often the determination of alternatives and the optimal solution depends primarily on the expertise, experience, and intuition of the Project Manager and the project team. This highlights the importance of project planning and the creation of effective project plans. The planning process tends to immerse the Project Manager and project team into the details of the project, which is very useful when quick and effective decisions are needed to resolve issues.

Case Study Update: Resolving Issues

They start as a trickle, become a steady stream, and turn into a tsunami—problems! To Sophie, it seemed like every day there was something new going wrong. The problems were coming from all angles. The execution of the project has just started and already the following problems have occurred:

- The Deco Productions company logo on the trade show banner is too small.
- The trade show banner stand is not available.
- The price of the giveaways (i.e., the postcards) is 40% more than budgeted.
- The demo version from the Development project team is late—these are usually sent as part of the media outreach.
- The first version of the multimedia demo isn't working as planned—the user experience is not very effective.
- The main actor signed for the promotional video was diagnosed with pneumonia and may need to be replaced.

During past projects, Sophie tried to solve each problem as they appeared. While this worked for small projects early in her career, on larger projects she became overwhelmed with issues and couldn't solve them as they arose. She would start to lose track of the status of the problem, which further compounded the issue. Now this seems to be happening again on this project.

Luckily, Sophie has developed a process that helps her manage the torrent of problems that often occur. As each issue is identified, she records the key information in an Issue Log that she keeps in a spreadsheet on her laptop before she tries to solve it. This has really helped her to keep track of each issue and to prioritize them so that she and the team are working on the most important issues first.

For small, frequent issues, Sophie has learned to trust her instinct. With the knowledge gained during the planning of the project, along with past experience, she's found that she's able to solve most problems quickly and effectively. For larger issues, she uses a formal method of determining the alternatives and then selecting the optimal solution.

Sophie has found that problems and issues can be very disruptive to the project team. Some team members assume the worst and develop a negative outlook for the project, which can affect the morale of the entire team. To minimize this, Sophie encourages each team member to follow the problem-solving process. Taking a systematic approach to resolving issues tends to reduce the negative emotions by focusing the team on alternatives and solutions.

The six new issues that were added to the project's Issue Log are shown below. Note that these are in addition to the existing issues of the project.

Issue Log

ISSUE LOG			
Project Name			
DCV4Launch–DecoCam V4 Product Launch			
Issue #	**Description**	**Priority**	**Status**
13	The Deco Productions company logo on the trade show banner is too small.	Medium	Not started
14	The trade show banner stand is not available.	Medium	Not started
15	The price of the giveaways (i.e., the postcards) is 40% more than budgeted. • Chris verified that the original estimate was too low. No further action to be taken.	Low	NPW
16	The demo version from the Development project team is late—these are usually sent as part of the media outreach. • Sophie requested more information from the project manager of the Development project team. Sarah will consider alternatives once this information is received.	Medium	Started
17	The first version of the multimedia demo isn't working as planned—the user experience is not very effective. • Decision made to upgrade the demo software to a newer version. • Chris tested the new version and resolved the issue.	High	Complete
18	The main actor signed for the promotional video was diagnosed with pneumonia and may need to be replaced. • Decision made to hire a new actor. • Maddy is working with the Resource Manager to hire a new actor.	High	Started

Using spreadsheet software, the Issue Log can be easily sorted according to the priority and/or status columns. For example, the Issue Log could be sorted from high to low priority issues.

MANAGING PROJECT CHANGE

Once a project's plans are completed and approved, any potential additions or modifications to the plan should be considered to be a change. It is very common to make changes during a project. As a project progresses, the business environment often changes, unexpected problems occur, activities take longer than expected, and new ideas are suggested. It can sometimes seem that the project is in a constant state of change.

Changes should be viewed as generally disruptive to the project's execution. Each time a change is made, plans need to be updated and work may need to be redone. Changes can introduce errors to the project, particularly those made quickly or at the last minute. Changes may also dampen the mood of the project team, as they may become increasingly uncertain about whether further changes will be coming.

However, this does not imply that the goal should be a complete elimination of change. There may be changes that are vital, perhaps based on new information that was not previously available.

The challenge is to determine the changes that should be implemented because they are beneficial to the project and those that should not be implemented because they are not beneficial enough to disrupt the project. To help make this determination, a **change control process** should be developed.

As part of developing a change control process, a person or group who will approve changes should be identified. Normally, this would include the Project Sponsor. However, in some large projects, this could be performed by a committee of individuals from across the organization.

For changes that are proposed during a project, the following steps are performed:

1. A **Change Request** is submitted by the person requesting the change. This request should include the following information:
    -   A description of the requested change
    -   A description of the potential benefit to the project resulting from the change

2. The Change Request is submitted to the Project Manager. The Project Manager, in consultation with project team members, assesses any impacts to the project including:
    -   an increase in the cost of the project;
    -   a delay to the end date of the project or other milestones;
    -   a change to the capabilities of the delivered outcomes of the project;
    -   a change to the level of risk present for the project.

3. The information contained in the first two steps is presented to the person or committee that approves the changes. This may be done either as the change is requested or on a periodic basis (e.g., weekly). Based on a comparison of the benefits and impact, a decision is made to either to approve or reject the change.

4. If the change is approved, the appropriate planning documents should be updated to reflect the change (e.g., project schedule, Project Scope Statement) and the work should be performed as required. If not approved, the person requesting the change should be informed.

The following is the template for a Change Request:

Change Request Template

CHANGE REQUEST FORM	
Project Name	[This section contains the project name that should appear consistently on all project documents. Organizations often have project naming conventions.]
Requested By	[Name of the person requesting the change.]
Request Date	[The date this form was submitted.]
Part A. Description of the Requested Change (Completed by the Requestor)	
[Complete description of the requested change to the project.]	
Part B. Benefit of the Requested Change (Completed by the Requestor)	
[Complete description of the benefit to the project if the requested change is made.]	
Part C. Impacts to the Project (Completed by the Project Manager)	
[Full description of the impact to the project's scope, quality, schedule, cost, risk, etc.]	
Part D. Change Request Decision (Completed by the Project Change Committee)	
[An indication of whether the change is approved in full, approved in part, or rejected.]	

Case Study Update: Managing Project Change

Just as Sophie arrives in the morning, Chris Sandburg, the Graphic Designer assigned to the project, walks into her office. He begins talking excitedly about this great idea that came to him on the way to work.

"Instead of producing postcards for the trade show giveaways, why don't we change them to look like picture frames? This will support the idea that DecoCam can do more than make a postcard."

Even though the timing is very tight to make this change, Sophie asks Chris to fill out a Change Request so that the idea will be considered as soon as possible.

That afternoon, Sophie checks her email inbox and notices that she has received another request for a possible change. In the email, the Project Manager of the DecoCam V4 Development project indicates that a special version of the DecoCam software could be created and used in the multimedia demo, providing a superior experience for the trade show participants. In her reply, Sophie thanks her for sending the idea and asks her to complete a Change Request.

Both requests are received later that day. Due to the tight timing, Sophie meets with her team members immediately in order to develop accurate estimates of the potential impact of making each change.

The next day, the weekly Project Change Committee meets. The members of the committee are Sophie Featherstone, the Project Manager; Arun Singh, the Project Sponsor; and Jason Brown, the Business Analyst. The committee reviews both Change Requests and discusses the pros and cons of each at length. The postcard/picture frame change request is approved, as the committee feels that the benefit is significant for a relatively modest cost. While they are tempted by the benefits of the multimedia request, they feel that the cost and the risk of errors occurring at the trade show are just not worth it. Therefore, this request is not approved.

After the meeting, Sophie checks her notes and makes the appropriate changes to the project plans. The Project Scope Statement is updated to reflect the change in scope and the Project Budget is updated to reflect the change in the project cost. The project schedule is not affected.

The following are the two Change Request forms that were created:

Change Request (Postcard)

CHANGE REQUEST FORM	
Project Name	DCV4Launch–DecoCam V4 Product Launch
Requested By	Chris Sandburg
Request Date	April 7, 2020
Part A. Description of the Requested Change (Completed by the Requestor)	
Change the trade show giveaways to resemble a picture frame rather than a postcard.	
Part B. Benefit of the Requested Change (Completed by the Requestor)	
A picture frame would more accurately demonstrate the benefit of the DecoCam software—it would allow the user to take outstanding pictures that would subsequently be framed. A postcard may be confusing as it suggests a travel theme which is unrelated to DecoCam.	

Continued

Part C. Impacts to the Project
(Completed by the Project Manager)

The impacts to the project are as follows:
• No change to the work effort or project schedule.
• The supplier could produce a card that would resemble a picture frame. The unit cost would increase from $1.00 to $1.20. For the 2,000 cards that will be ordered, this results in a $400 budget increase to order the cards.
• No change in the quality.
• No change to the risk.

Part D. Change Request Decision
(Completed by the Project Change Committee)

The Project Change Committee approved this request. The picture frame trade show giveaway will be more effective and memorable than the postcard. This benefit outweighed the $400 cost increase.

Change Request (Modified Multimedia Demo)

CHANGE REQUEST FORM	
Project Name	DCV4Launch–DecoCam V4 Product Launch
Requested By	Zoe Purdie
Request Date	April 7, 2020

Part A. Description of the Requested Change
(Completed by the Requestor)

Develop a modified version of the DecoCam V4 software to be used in the trade show multimedia demo.

Part B. Benefit of the Requested Change
(Completed by the Requestor)

The modified version would have restricted functionality but would allow the user to fully experience the system, rather than using the simulated slideshow application that is currently being planned.

Part C. Impacts to the Project
(Completed by the Project Manager)

The impacts to the project are as follows:
• The modified version of the software could be completed for $6,000.
• No change to the project schedule.
• There is an increased risk that the new software contains errors that become evident during the trade show.

Part D. Change Request Decision
(Completed by the Project Change Committee)

The Project Change Committee rejected this request. While the potential for this modified software is appealing, the increased cost would cause the project to exceed its $60,000 budget. As well, the increased potential for problems at the trade show is not acceptable.

CHAPTER SUMMARY

Key Concepts

1. Projects are rarely executed completely according to plan and therefore processes are needed to manage the disruptions that occur.
2. Project issues should be documented and prioritized in an Issue Log and then subsequently resolved.
3. A change control process should be developed to ensure all requested changes to the plan are managed effectively.

Key Terminology

Change Control Process: A formal process to approve or reject proposed changes to the project.

Change Request: A document containing information related to a proposed project change that is used during the change control process.

Issue: A condition or situation that, if left unresolved, will reduce the performance or effectiveness of the project.

Issue Log: A document containing information about the project issues that have occurred.

DISCUSSION QUESTIONS

1. The problem-solving process described in this chapter could be viewed as being slow and ponderous by some who might want to just "do something" quickly. How would you respond to this viewpoint?
2. Do all issues result in change requests? Explain why issues would and would not require the change control process.
3. When developing a change control process, who should approve the proposed changes? Describe the factors that should be considered when making this decision.
4. Perform an online search to research project issues. Summarize five common issues that occur during projects.

13 Managing the Human Resources Aspects of the Project

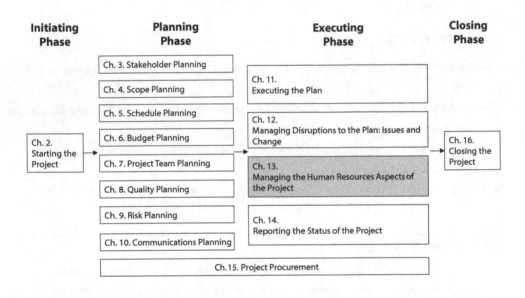

Initiating Phase	Planning Phase	Executing Phase	Closing Phase
	Ch. 3. Stakeholder Planning	Ch. 11. Executing the Plan	
	Ch. 4. Scope Planning		
	Ch. 5. Schedule Planning	Ch. 12. Managing Disruptions to the Plan: Issues and Change	
Ch. 2. Starting the Project	Ch. 6. Budget Planning		Ch. 16. Closing the Project
	Ch. 7. Project Team Planning	Ch. 13. Managing the Human Resources Aspects of the Project	
	Ch. 8. Quality Planning		
	Ch. 9. Risk Planning	Ch. 14. Reporting the Status of the Project	
	Ch. 10. Communications Planning		
	Ch. 15. Project Procurement		

INTRODUCTION TO MANAGING THE HUMAN RESOURCES ASPECTS OF THE PROJECT

Projects are performed by people (the project team) for people (the project stakeholders). The way that each of these groups interacts has a tremendous bearing on the success of the project. It is therefore important to focus on the management of the people aspects of the project.

In order for a project to be successful, Project Managers need to accomplish the objectives of the project through the work of others. This involves actions such as assigning work to be completed, making decisions, achieving consensus, and resolving conflict.

In many organizations, the Project Manager has the responsibility to complete the project, but often lacks the positional power of others in the organization, such as the Directors and Vice-Presidents. Team members are assigned to the project team but do not always report directly to the Project Manager. In order to function effectively in this environment, Project Managers will benefit from an understanding of **power** and **influence** and their effective use.

UNDERSTANDING POWER AND INFLUENCE

Power is the capacity to influence others to change their attitude and behaviour. People possess power based on a number of sources. Research performed by J. R. P. French and B. H. Raven (1959) identified the following five sources of power[1]:

- Expertise: power based on people's perception of the leader's knowledge and expertise
- Referent: power based on people's desire to be identified with the leader
- Legitimate: power based on the leader's formal position within an organization
- Reward: power based on the leader's ability to provide resources, pay raises, promotions, etc., to others
- Coercive: power based on the leader's ability to penalize others or withdraw privileges

As already discussed, Project Managers have limited legitimate power and therefore cannot generally rely heavily on this source. A Project Manager's reward power will be restricted by the project budget and is therefore limited. Power through coercive methods is generally only used in rare circumstances and is not recommended as an ongoing approach.

This leaves expertise and referent power as the key sources of power for Project Managers. Project Managers may increase their expert power by adopting an attitude of continuous learning and by understanding the knowledge they require in order to effectively manage a project. Referent power may be developed through a number of approaches, including the effective use of communication, interpersonal skills, honesty, and ethical behaviour.

Influence is the exercise of power to bring about change. There are many tactics that may be used to influence people, such as:

- engaging others in rational or logical explanations (convincing based on sound reasoning);

- inspiring others with a higher purpose or vision;
- interpersonal skills and acts of friendship or kindness;
- involving others in the planning process and seeking out their advice;
- demonstrating the advantage of cooperation.

The amount of power that someone possesses directly affects the degree to which they are able to influence others. For example, someone with recognized expertise in a subject area (expert power) will likely be able to successfully influence others in regards to this subject, compared to someone who lacks this expertise.

Project Managers should be continually considering and developing their sources of power given how it affects their ability to influence others involved in the project. The use of power and influence better enables the Project Manager to manage the project team, manage stakeholder relationships, and resolve conflict during the project.

Case Study Update: Understanding Power and Influence

Periodically, Sophie reflects on her work experience prior to becoming a Project Manager. Her background is in business communications and her first job at Deco Productions was as a Communication Specialist.

Once she became a Project Manager, she assumed that because of her position, she could just tell people what to do and they would do it. However, because her team members didn't report directly to her (they reported to other managers in the organization), she quickly realized that she lacked this type of positional power.

She shudders when she thinks of some of her early projects. On one project, she set up a series of deadlines and pointed out team members who didn't meet the deadline in the weekly team meeting. She quickly found that her team members felt they were being publicly shamed in front of their teammates and were being punished for delays that were often beyond their control. Instead of motivating the team, they were becoming hostile to her. On another project, she decided to give out small bonuses and gift certificates whenever team members achieved something exceptional. But then she found that team members started to expect a bonus and were demotivated if they didn't receive it. In addition, she exceeded her discretionary budget halfway through the project.

Over time, she came to realize that she shouldn't rely on the use of rewards or disciplinary actions to influence her team. Instead, she found that her team would be much more likely to perform effectively if she gained their confidence and respect. She now focuses on activities such as:

- interacting with each team member on a personal level;
- involving team members in the decision-making process;
- being flexible and open to new ideas, including admitting when she is wrong;
- clearly communicating the reasons for project decisions and actions.

The results of her efforts have been positive. Team members see her not only as a competent Project Manager, but also as a reasonable and fair person. Sophie learned the hard way how important power and influence can be when managing people. She keeps these strategies in mind as she completes her current project.

MANAGING THE PROJECT TEAM

The stakeholder group that normally requires the Project Manager's greatest attention is the project team. Managing the team consists of the following two functions:
- Managing the team's activities
- Building the team's capabilities

Managing the Project Team's Activities

An important aspect of the Project Manager role is to manage the performance of team members as they complete the work of the project. P. Hersey, K. Blanchard, and D. Johnson (1996) theorized that the management style used should match the characteristics of the team member.[2] That is, Project Managers should vary their approach depending on the expertise of each team member as follows:
- For team members with a low-level of expertise, a directive management style may be used. This would involve close supervision, including providing direct instructions and frequent reviews of their work.
- For team members with a low to medium level of expertise, a coaching management style may be used. This would involve less supervision, with the Project Manager guiding and supporting the team member.
- For team members with a medium to high level of expertise, a supportive management style may be used. Very little supervision and direction are required, with support and encouragement provided as needed.
- For team members with a high level of expertise, responsibility may be delegated to the team member with very little involvement required by the Project Manager, other than periodic updates.

During projects, particularly those with long durations, the expertise levels of team members may change during the project.

The use of the Project's Manager's power and influence will be important for the effective completion of the work assignments. During the project, there will be many interactions between the Project Manager and team members where additional work may be required, an additional approach may be suggested, or a new issue may need to be solved.

Case Study Update: Managing the Project Team's Activities

Sophie studies the project schedule, reviewing which team members are assigned to each project activity. During a recent team meeting, the schedule was distributed to all team members to ensure that everyone was aware of their own activities.

However, this isn't the end of Sophie's involvement. She considers each of her team members and how she should manage them:

- The Communications Specialist: the company has recently hired Sarah and while she's eager to learn, she's also very inexperienced. Sophie will work very closely with her, helping her draft a daily to-do list and encouraging her to ask questions as they arise.
- The Marketing Specialist: Maddy has been in her current position for over a year and is becoming comfortable in her role. She makes a mental note to drop by to see her every few days to provide support as needed.
- The Graphic Designer: Chris has extensive experience. Unless he asks a question or raises an issue, Sophie does not need to spend additional time with him.

She continues this process with each of the remaining team members. She feels confident about her planned interaction with each team member, as she'll be able to provide the right amount of time and support for their needs.

Building the Project Team's Capabilities

The goal of the Project Manager should be to help team members achieve a higher state of expertise and productivity. This benefits the project in a number of ways, including increased output, lower costs, and higher quality deliverables.

The expertise and productivity of team members will generally improve without intervention, as the completion of the work itself will increase a team member's experience. This can be enhanced through the following:

- The team member may undergo training, either formally within a class-room or online course, or informally through on-the-job mentoring. Time may be set aside in the project schedule for training.
- Regular feedback should be provided, particularly for team members with lower levels of expertise. This may take the form of day-to-day informal feedback or regularly scheduled formal appraisals.

The Project Manager should also create a positive environment for the project team to effectively perform. Timely recognition of an individual's or team's accomplishments can be a powerful motivator for increased performance. This recognition may be financial (e.g., bonus, paid lunch) or non-financial (e.g., thanking the team for their efforts).

The Project Manager should also consider the use of team building activities to create an effective team environment. Team building activites may be informal (e.g., fostering an open door policy) or organized (e.g., organizing an occasional team lunch or social event). Activities such as these are helpful as teams usually perform more effectively as their familiarity with each other increases.

Case Study Update: Building the Project Team's Capabilities

As she organizes her project team, Sophie's thoughts turn to the performance of her team. She knows that the success of the project is tied to how well her team performs individually and as a group.

Deco Productions supports the team members' ongoing skills training by sending employees to take courses as needed. Sophie also knows that on-the-job training takes place during her projects and she allots time for this within her project schedule.

While these training opportunities will improve individual performance, Sophie knows that the group also needs to perform effectively as a team. She recalls one of her projects from a couple of years ago when it looked like she had a very strong team. Each person assigned to her project was competent in their respective fields. However, once the project was underway, Sophie realized that something was wrong. The team seemed to act more like a group of strangers, and the reduced communication and cooperation between them began to negatively affect the project. She also found that the team became consumed by the amount of work required and the project issues, creating a dark cloud over the project. The end result was a failed project with many of the team members blaming each other for the failure.

For the DecoCam project, a number of the team members do not know each other well, so there is a chance that history could repeat itself. Sophie plans to gather her team

Continued

at a local restaurant and pay for the first couple of appetizers. It will serve as an informal project kickoff and help the team members to get to know each other outside of the day-to-day work.

Additionally, Sophie likes to begin her team meetings with humorous stories about the latest thing that her four-year-old daughter said or some unlikely situation that occurred during a family outing. Often, other team members share their own stories as well. This tends to bring the team closer together, lightens the mood, and creates a positive environment for the team to tackle the challenges in front of them.

Sophie hopes these types of team building activities will help her avoid the pitfalls of the previous project.

MANAGING THE STAKEHOLDER RELATIONSHIPS

In addition to the project team, the Project Manager also interacts with a number of other project stakeholders during the project. During project planning, an analysis of the project stakeholders and the development of a Stakeholder Management Plan were completed.

As the project is executed, each of the stakeholders should be actively managed, using the Stakeholder Management Plan as a reference. As with the management of team members, the Project Manager's power and use of influence is extremely important, especially since many project stakeholders often possess more legitimate power than the Project Manager.

Case Study Update: Managing the Stakeholder Relationships

It's the end of a long week and the pace of the project is increasing significantly. At this point, it can be easy to get swept up into the urgent daily activities of the project.

Even though she is busy, Sophie spends a few minutes each week considering her ongoing relationship with the project stakeholders. She pulls up the Stakeholder Management Plan on her laptop to review her planned actions with each stakeholder. It's been updated numerous times throughout the project as Sophie gains a greater understanding of the project and its stakeholders.

Looking at the plan, she jots down a couple of new entries to her daily to-do list. She hasn't dropped by to see Casey lately, so she adds this to the list. She also realizes that there have been a few changes to her schedule and she should send an update to the other DecoCam Project Managers.

After a few additional updates to the Stakeholder Management Plan, she saves the file and closes her laptop. Looking at her to-do list, she decides to head to Casey's office first.

MANAGING CONFLICT

Having the goal of creating something unique in a finite period of time with a limited budget can lead to situations where conflict is very likely. Disagreements are common during projects, both within the project team and with project stakeholders.

Some level of conflict is productive for a project. A moderate level of disagreement is a sign that stakeholders are able to provide input to the project, and these discussions can result in superior project designs and solutions. However, a high level of conflict can cause the project to become unproductive.

As with each section of this chapter, the Project Manager's power and use of influence are important as conflict management relies heavily on communication and interpersonal relationships.

R. R. Blake and J. S. Mouton (1964) created the following model to manage conflict.[3] For any given situation where conflict exists, there are two characteristics that need to be determined:

- The importance of the situation (rated from low to high): some situations causing conflict are fairly minor or trivial while others may be extremely critical.
- The importance of maintaining the relationship between the people involved in the conflict (rated from low to high): in some situations, when the people will continue to work together during the current and future projects, the importance of maintaining the relationship would likely be high. On the other hand, when future contact is unlikely or in emergency situations, the importance would likely be low.

Once these two characteristics are determined, a suitable conflict management approach can be chosen. There are five conflict management approaches that may be used.

Collaborating Approach

The collaborating approach is recommended for highly important situations where the importance of the ongoing relationship is also high. The recommended approach involves collaboration in which both parties work together to develop a solution.

Accommodating Approach

A common conflict management mistake that is made is to attempt to win every argument regardless of the importance of the situation. However, there are often disagreements where the situation is relatively unimportant, but the importance of the ongoing relationship is high. In these instances, accommodating the other person's viewpoint is recommended, especially if they view the situation as being important. Not only does this eliminate the conflict, but it also tends to generate goodwill that may be useful for future interactions.

Directing Approach

In some cases, the importance of the situation is high and the importance of the relationship is low. This would apply to situations such as emergencies or the enforcement of company policies. In these cases, a directing approach is recommended in which the decision is made without input from the other party.

Avoiding Approach

In some cases, the situation and the ongoing relationship are unimportant. These tend to be time wasters—the disagreements arise about something that neither party is concerned about. In these cases, it is best to avoid the conflict altogether by not participating.

Compromising Approach

Often, potential conflicts do not fit neatly into a model where the importance (of the situation or relationship) is either high or low. In some cases, it is either unclear or of medium importance. In these cases, a compromise may be made where each side concedes something in order to achieve an agreement.

Compromise varies from collaboration in that compromise involves finding a middle ground, while collaboration involves developing alternate solutions and possibilities. Compromise is generally quicker to perform than collaboration. The end result of collaboration may be the realization that a compromise is the best alternative.

Managing conflict is important during projects because if it is not addressed, it will likely affect not only the situation causing the conflict, but also the on-going stakeholder relationships. Stakeholder management is important because each of the conflict management approaches is more easily and effectively implemented if there is a strong relationship with the stakeholders involved.

Additionally, for each of the conflict management approaches, the use of appropriate interpersonal skills is beneficial. For example, the directing approach does not imply that the interpersonal style should be harsh. An open and respectful interpersonal style is recommended regardless of which approach is chosen.

Case Study Update: Managing Conflict

One of the things that Sophie didn't realize when she became a Project Manager was the number of disagreements that would occur. At times, by the end of the week, she feels like a referee! But over time, by analyzing the characteristics of each new conflict, she's having more success with conflict management.

Just this week, there were two potential conflicts with her Project Sponsor. Arun is a key stakeholder of the project and maintaining a positive relationship with him is very important. The first conflict arose because Arun felt strongly that the project should be completed one week earlier so that the marketing team would be able to create a better marketing plan for the DecoCam V4 project. Sophie saw this as a very significant change that could affect the budget of the project and add significant risk as well. To address this conflict, she booked a meeting with Arun where they explored each of their concerns and searched for possible solutions. In the end, they settled on a new approach: the original project due date will be maintained, but Sophie will meet with the marketing team one week before this due date to present all of the product launch deliverables. By using a collaborative approach, both Sophie and Arun were satisfied with the resolution.

The second conflict had to do with the weekly status report. As part of the Communication Management Plan, Arun receives a weekly status report sent as an electronic file attached to an email. Arun recently requested that Sophie also sends him a printed copy of the report. Sophie sighed when she received the request, as this is just one more thing she would need to do each week. In addition, the company policy has been to reduce paper use wherever possible. However, when she thinks about it, this issue really isn't important to her, and apparently it's important to Arun. Therefore, she accommodates the request by adding this extra step to her weekly processes.

Also during the week, Sophie ran into a situation with her project team. During a team meeting, Sarah and Eli said that rather than recording the number of hours that they worked on the project on a daily basis, they would prefer to estimate their hours at the

Continued

end of the project. Sophie explained why having current information on a regular basis is useful to her effective management of the project. This satisfied Sarah, but Eli digs in and states that he still doesn't want to record his hours during the project. Given the high importance of timely project information and that this is a company policy that cannot be changed, Sophie takes a directing approach and lets Eli know that while she understands his concerns, it must be done.

A day later, one of the employees from the Finance department drops by her office. It seems that her team was "very loud" as they celebrated the completion of a key milestone earlier in the week. She asks Sophie to speak to her team to make sure they are quiet next time. Sophie recalls that she was probably laughing the loudest at the meeting. Overall, she feels that this issue is somewhat trivial since it was a very brief period of celebrating and they didn't exceed the normal noise levels in the office. She also doesn't know the employee and probably won't have any further interactions with her. She thanks the employee for the feedback but politely indicates that she won't be pursuing this further. By avoiding any further discussion, she limits the time spent on this issue. She doesn't expect to hear any more about it.

And finally, while meeting with the Project Managers of the other DecoCam V4 projects, two of the Project Managers asked if the Project Status Report could be sent to them by 8:00 a.m. on Thursdays, rather than by noon. They would like more time to prepare for the Friday meeting. This concerns Sophie, as she usually arrives to the office at 8:30 a.m. after dropping her daughter off at daycare. She feels that it's not an overly important issue though she knows that maintaining a good relationship with the other Project Managers is important. They reach a compromise that the Project Status Report will be sent by 10:00 a.m.

By the end of the week, Sophie feels she effectively managed each of the conflicts that came up. She is sure, though, that there will be more problems to address next week.

CHAPTER SUMMARY

Key Concepts

1. Since the Project Manager role often lacks the explicit authority of senior management, it is vital to exert other forms of power and influence.
2. During execution, the Project Manager manages the team members' activities and develops their capabilities.
3. Building on the Stakeholder Management Plan developed during planning, the Project Manager continues to develop stakeholder relationships throughout the Executing Phase.

4. The Project Manager should assess and manage conflict between project stakeholders to ensure the effective execution of the project.

Key Terminology

Influence: The exercise of power to bring about change.

Power: The capacity to influence others to change their attitude and behaviour.

DISCUSSION QUESTIONS

1. Review the five sources of power. Which one do you think is your greatest source of power? Which is the weakest?
2. Consider the different approaches to influence others mentioned in this chapter. What approach do you use most often? Is there another approach that would be more effective?
3. Think of a recent conflict that you were involved in. What approach did you use to manage the conflict? According to the conflict management model, what approach should have been used?
4. Perform an online search to research project team development. List any additional team development ideas that you find beyond those described in this chapter.

NOTES

1. French, J. R. P., & Raven, B. H. (1959). "The Bases of Social Power." In *Studies of Social Power*, ed. D. Cartwright. Institute for Social Research. Ann Arbor, MI.
2. Hersey, P., Blanchard, K., & Johnson, D. (1996). *Management of Organizational Behaviour: Utilizing Human Resources*. Prentice Hall, Upper Saddle River, NJ.
3. Blake, R. R., & Mouton, J. S. (1964). *The Managerial Grid*. Gulf Publishing Company, Houston, TX.

14 Reporting the Status of the Project

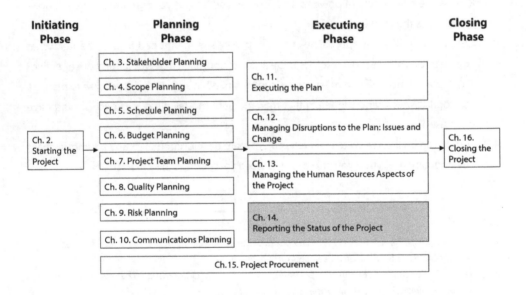

Initiating Phase	Planning Phase	Executing Phase	Closing Phase
	Ch. 3. Stakeholder Planning	Ch. 11. Executing the Plan	
	Ch. 4. Scope Planning		
	Ch. 5. Schedule Planning	Ch. 12. Managing Disruptions to the Plan: Issues and Change	
Ch. 2. Starting the Project	Ch. 6. Budget Planning		Ch. 16. Closing the Project
	Ch. 7. Project Team Planning	Ch. 13. Managing the Human Resources Aspects of the Project	
	Ch. 8. Quality Planning		
	Ch. 9. Risk Planning	Ch. 14. Reporting the Status of the Project	
	Ch. 10. Communications Planning		
	Ch. 15. Project Procurement		

INTRODUCTION TO REPORTING THE STATUS OF THE PROJECT

Throughout a project, the progress made often varies from the project plan. At any time, the project may be ahead of or behind schedule, under or over budget, and more or less of the project scope may be completed. It is the nature of the planning process that there is some level of variance between the planned progress and the actual progress of the project.

However, it is important that the Project Manager and project stakeholders are aware of this variance. An accurate assessment of the project's current status allows the Project Manager to implement correcting measures as needed.

The status of the project is documented in a Project Status Report. For most projects, a weekly status report is recommended. The Project Status Report enhances the communication between the project team and the stakeholders. Many stakeholders are not involved in the day-to-day activities of the project, so the Project Status Report serves as their main window into the project.

THE PROJECT STATUS REPORTING PROCESS

The Project Status Report is produced by the Project Manager in consultation with the project team. To produce this report, the following steps need to be completed:

1. Identify the overall status of the project. While projects often have various positive and negative occurrences, it is important to report the overall condition of the project to provide clarity to the Project Sponsor and other stakeholders. A common method is to select one of following colours to describe the status of the project:

    · Green: this status indicates the project is on schedule to achieve its objectives according to the project plan.

    · Yellow: this status indicates the project is underperforming and there is some risk that the project will not achieve its objectives according to the plan.

    · Red: this status indicates the project is experiencing significant problems and there is a high level of risk that the project will not achieve its objectives according to the plan.

2. List the activities that the team members worked on during the past week, even if the work was not completed.

3. List the activities that the team members plan to work on during the next week of the project. Note that the same activity may be listed in steps 2 and 3. For example, if an activity started during the past week and will continue into next week, then it would be listed in each section.

4. List the current project issues. The Project Manager should review the list of outstanding issues and determine those issues that should be included on the status report. Some issues may not be significant enough to share with stakeholders outside of the project team.

5. List the recent changes to the project. Any changes that were approved using the project's change management process since the last status report should be listed.

The template for the Project Status Report is as follows:

Project Status Report Template

PROJECT STATUS REPORT	
Project Name	[This section contains the project name that should appear consistently on all project documents. Organizations often have project naming conventions.]
For Week Ending	[Date of the report. Record the end date of the past week.]
Project Status	[Green, Yellow, or Red.]
Status Description	[Provide an overview of the project's current status. If the status is yellow or red, indicate: • The reason(s) that the status is yellow or red. • The planned action(s) that will bring the project back to a green status.]

Activities—During the Past Week

[List all activities that the team members worked on during the past week of the project.]

Activities—Planned for Next Week

[List all activities that the team members will work on during the next week of the project.]

Project Issues

[List any issues from the Issue Log that are significant and should be shared with the audience of this report. If any related work has been done or decisions have been made, a summary should be provided.]

Project Changes

[List any project changes that were approved since the last report.]

Case Study Update: Reporting the Status of the Project

Sophie is running late this morning, as it took a little longer than expected to drop her daughter off at daycare. Without bothering to take her coat off, she heads directly to the daily project team huddle.

On Thursday mornings, the main purpose of the meeting is to determine the current status of the project so that Sophie can complete the weekly Project Status Report. Her first question is always the same: "Is the project where it needs to be to be completed successfully?" This usually results in some debate before a team consensus emerges.

Sophie then reviews the work of the past week listed on the schedule. Each team member reports whether the work was completed or if any work remains to be done. Likewise, the work scheduled for the coming week is reviewed. Various comments are made regarding the viability of the plan and the possible adjustments needed. Sophie keeps notes on what is said throughout the meeting.

Next, any outstanding issues are reviewed, which often generates some lively discussion among the team. And finally, Sophie ensures that the team is aware of any changes that were approved during the past week.

Sophie encourages the team to be completely transparent when reporting status updates. She wants them to be as accurate as possible in their reporting and she certainly does not want them to cover up any problems that may occur. While a yellow or red status is not desirable as it attracts the attention of the Project Sponsor and other stakeholders, it allows Sophie to request additional resources if needed. In turn, the management of Deco Productions needs this early warning system in order to respond with assistance as required.

Early on in the discussion, it becomes clear that the project currently has a yellow status. The unresolved budget issue and the need to hire a new actor for the promotional video are both significant concerns.

As the discussion proceeds, Sophie updates the Project Status Report on her laptop. As documented in the Communication Management Plan, she needs to send this report to the Project Sponsor and other DecoCam V4 Project Managers by 10:00 a.m. in preparation for the Project Status Review Meeting on Friday.

Sophie likes to involve the project team in the creation of the Project Status Report not only because they are providing the information for the status updates, but also because it benefits the team to understand the current status of the project as a whole. Following the meeting, Sophie makes sure that any required updates are made to the project plans based on the team meeting. She then makes a few final edits to the Project Status Report and sends it to Arun and the other Project Managers. A quick glance at her watch shows that the time is 9:55 a.m. Smiling to herself, she is reminded why Thursday mornings are always very busy.

Based on this work, the following Project Status Report is produced.

Project Status Report

PROJECT STATUS REPORT	
Project Name	DCV4Launch–DecoCam V4 Product Launch
For Week Ending	Friday, April 10, 2020
Project Status	Yellow
Status Description	The work of the project is proceeding well, with all tasks currently on schedule. The project is reporting a yellow project status for two main reasons: 1. The project is currently $820 over budget. 2. The first issue listed below (i.e., the need to hire a new video actor) could potentially delay the completion of the promotional video. The source of the budget increase is being investigated—more information to come. A high priority has been placed on acquiring a new actor as soon as possible.

Activities—During the Past Week

Create sign graphics/text.

Order banner stands.

Create holograph cards.

Create social media strategy.

Develop social media content.

Develop video concept.

Develop video storyboard.

Activities—Planned for Next Week

Create holographic cards.

Order cards.

Create mural for booth.

Update product page.

Create online slideshow.

Create outreach list.

Project Issues
The main actor who was signed for the promotional video was recently diagnosed with pneumonia. The decision was made to hire a new actor.
The demo version from the Development project team is late—this is usually sent as part of the media outreach. More information has been requested from the Development team's project manager.
The Deco Productions company logo on the tradeshow banner is too small. No progress has been made on this issue.
The trade show banner stand selected is not available. No progress has been made on this issue.

Project Changes
The trade show giveaways will be changed to resemble a picture frame rather than a postcard.

CHAPTER SUMMARY

Key Concepts

1. It is important for all stakeholders to be aware of the current status of the project and any variance from the project plans. The Project Status Report is usually produced on a weekly basis.

2. The project status reporting process is as follows:
   i. Identify the overall status of the project as green, yellow, or red.
   ii. List the activities that occurred during the past week.
   iii. List the activities that are planned to occur next week.
   iv. List the current project issues.
   v. List the recent changes to the project.

DISCUSSION QUESTIONS

1. When indicating the overall status of the project, the colour green, yellow, or red is selected. Should combinations of colours also be allowed? For example, a status between yellow and red could be labelled as orange. Discuss the pros and cons of this approach.

2. Project Status Reports are usually produced on a weekly basis. Should they be produced more frequently or less frequently? Discuss the pros and cons of each.

3. Should all issues in the Issue Log be listed on the status report? What types of issues should potentially not be included?

4. Perform an online search to research examples of Project Status Reports. List any additional information not mentioned in this text that may be included in the report.

PART IV

PROJECT PROCUREMENT AND THE CLOSING PHASE

Up to this point in the text, the project management processes and tools have been presented with the assumption that all work will be completed within the same organization that receives the output of the project. While this is true for many projects, there is another classification of processes for projects in which one organization performs project work for another. This is known as project procurement. Internal projects and projects involving procurement share many processes and tools. Therefore, most of the concepts covered up to this point in the text apply to projects involving procurement. However, there are also some additional processes and tools to be explored.

Once all work is complete, whether for an internal project or a procurement project, the project moves to the Closing Phase of the project. While short in duration, it is important to ensure that the project is finished effectively.

15 Project Procurement

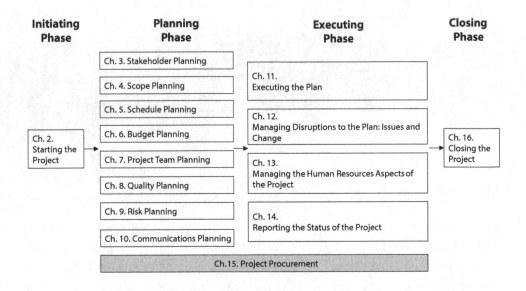

Initiating Phase	Planning Phase	Executing Phase	Closing Phase

- Ch. 2. Starting the Project
- Ch. 3. Stakeholder Planning
- Ch. 4. Scope Planning
- Ch. 5. Schedule Planning
- Ch. 6. Budget Planning
- Ch. 7. Project Team Planning
- Ch. 8. Quality Planning
- Ch. 9. Risk Planning
- Ch. 10. Communications Planning

- Ch. 11. Executing the Plan
- Ch. 12. Managing Disruptions to the Plan: Issues and Change
- Ch. 13. Managing the Human Resources Aspects of the Project
- Ch. 14. Reporting the Status of the Project

- Ch. 16. Closing the Project

Ch. 15. Project Procurement

INTRODUCTION TO PROJECT PROCUREMENT

During the case study project, employees of Deco Productions internal to the organization completed all of the work. However, on many projects, some portion of the work is performed externally by another organization. There are many reasons for work to be completed externally, including:

- the potential for lower cost or earlier delivery;
- gaining access to skills or knowledge not present internally;
- internal resources are not available.

The amount of work performed externally may be either a small or significant percentage of the total project. Terms used to describe this work include outsourcing, purchasing, and procurement.

Throughout the procurement process, there are two main parties: the **buyer** and the **seller**. The buyer is the organization that purchases the product, service, or result from another organization. The seller is the organization that produces the product, service, or result for sale to another organization.

The following are the stages of project procurement:

Stages of Project Procurement

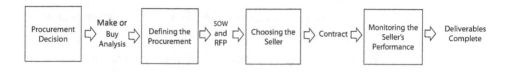

When planning the work of a project, an important decision is to determine the deliverables that will be created internally and the deliverables that will be created externally. A **Make or Buy Analysis** can help determine whether to "make" the project deliverables or "buy" the project deliverables.

If there are deliverables that will be created externally based on the results of the Make or Buy Analysis, the procurement process begins. During this stage, the procurement is defined in detail in the **Statement of Work** (SOW) and the **Request for Proposal** (RFP), which are described later in the chapter.

Once the SOW and RFP are produced, the process of choosing the seller begins. Once the seller is chosen, a **contract** is created and signed by both the buyer and the seller.

The final stage occurs when the seller produces the deliverables. The buyer's role is to monitor the seller's performance to ensure the work is performed according to the terms of the contract.

MAKE OR BUY ANALYSIS

When deciding whether to make or buy the deliverables for projects, it is useful to divide the deliverables into three categories:
- deliverables that will definitely be made internally;
- deliverables that will definitely be bought externally;
- deliverables that could be made internally or could be bought externally.

For projects that fall into the first two categories, the decision of whether the work should be performed internally or externally is obvious and no further analysis is required. For the first category, this may be work that has been traditionally performed within the organization. For the second, the organization may lack the expertise or the resources to perform this work.

However, for the third category, the decision of whether to perform the project work internally or externally is not obvious and therefore further analysis is required. This process, known as Make or Buy Analysis, consists of comparing the make option and the buy option according to the expected cost, quality, time required, and risk of each option.

Other factors may also affect this analysis. The buyer may currently lack the necessary resources to perform the work due to other projects or priorities. Or, the strategy of the buyer's organization could be changing to increase the amount of project work performed externally.

Case Study Update: Performing the Make or Buy Analysis

Early in the Planning Phase, Sophie reviews the Work Breakdown Structure of the project. As usual, time is limited and resources are scarce, so if there are any opportunities to outsource any of the work, now is the time to consider the options.

Most of the deliverables are typical of the work performed by Deco Productions and therefore will be produced internally. However, two deliverables catch Sophie's eye: the Multimedia Demo and Social Media. Both could potentially be performed externally, so further analysis is required.

Sophie first considers the Multimedia Demo. Enlisting help from her project team, the following analysis is completed:

Make or Buy Analysis—Multimedia Demo

CRITERIA	MAKE OPTION	BUY OPTION
Cost	Current estimate is $4,400.	The expected cost is $5,000.
Scope	Includes all scope.	Includes all scope.
Risk	There is a risk that Chris may be required to work on other projects and will not be able to complete this work as scheduled.	An external organization will not be as familiar with the DecoCam product. The quality may not be as high.

After further consideration and discussion with the Project Sponsor, the decision was made to outsource the production of the multimedia demo, despite the higher cost. The risk that Chris may be pulled onto another project was too high to ignore.

Next, Sophie considers the Social Media deliverable:

Make or Buy Analysis—Social Media

CRITERIA	MAKE OPTION	BUY OPTION
Cost	Current estimate is $2,400.	Expected cost is $2,400.
Scope	Includes all scope.	Includes all scope.
Risk	Moderate to low risk due to the marketing team's familiarity with the organization and product.	Lack of familiarity with the organization and product may increase the risk of lower-quality social media being produced.

After consulting with the Project Sponsor, Sophie decided that the social media work will not be outsourced and will remain with the project team. The risk of an external company producing lower quality social media posts was unacceptable to Sophie.

DEFINING THE PROCUREMENT

Once the buyer decides to procure work from outside the organization, the next challenge is to define the characteristics of the procurement in order for prospective sellers to understand the needs of the buyer.

This definition consists of two documents: the Statement of Work (SOW) and Request for Proposal (RFP).

The Statement of Work (SOW)

The purpose of the SOW is to completely describe the work to be completed during the procurement. Its content may vary depending on the type, size, and complexity of the project. However, the following type of information is typically contained in a SOW:
- Specifications of the work to be completed
- The required quantity
- The required quality or level of performance
- The period of performance for the work
- The location where the work will be performed
- Any other special requirements

The SOW may include other documents, such as design documents, schematics, and blueprints. It may also contain information contained in the Project Scope Statement.

The Request for Proposal (RFP)

The purpose of the RFP is to describe the process that prospective sellers will use to submit proposals to the buyer.

RFPs are used in situations where the proposals provided by the prospective sellers may contain unique solutions. In situations where the solutions of each seller are identical or very similar, a Request for Quote (RFQ) will be used. RFQs are commonly used for purchasing materials or other off-the-shelf items. In situations where the buyer is seeking information, a Request for Information (RFI) will be used. The remainder of this chapter will describe the use of an RFP.

As with the SOW, the content of an RFP will vary significantly depending on the type, size, and complexity of the project. The following is the type of information typically found in an RFP:

- Process details regarding how the prospective seller should submit their proposal, including the required information, format, number of copies, and the date and time that the proposal must be submitted
- The Statement of Work
- Any required contract provisions
- An indication of how the proposal will be evaluated (e.g., cost, quality)

The RFP and SOW should be considered a package that fully describes the project procurement to prospective sellers and therefore enables the seller to develop and submit a proposal.

Case Study Update: Defining the Procurement

With the decision to procure the Multimedia Demo from outside the organization, Sophie begins to develop two new documents: the Statement of Work and the Request for Proposal.

Sophie knows that the procurement process, especially for large procurements, can be a complex process. She finds that it is often advisable to seek out assistance from those with procurement expertise. At Deco Productions, they are usually found in the purchasing, supply chain, or logistics areas of the organization. She knows it is also important to obtain legal assistance, particularly at the point when the contract is created.

So, in order to have a successful procurement process, Sophie negotiates the assistance of representatives from the Supply Chain and Logistics Department, and the Legal Department. She asks each of the representatives to review her documentation and provide advice throughout the procurement process.

Given the amount of planning work that has been performed, creating the SOW is fairly straightforward. Using the WBS and Project Scope Statement as a guide, she describes the key features of the Multimedia Demo in detail. To ensure the demo is ready by the product launch date (May 8th), she is very specific about the due date for the work. Sophie also includes a number of technical requirements in the special requirements section of the SOW.

At the same time that she begins to work on the SOW, she starts to work on the RFP. Looking at the project schedule, she selects April 10th as the date that proposals must be submitted. The proposal itself should provide a description of the proposed Multimedia Demo, a cost estimate, and a list of the key milestones including the final delivery date. She indicates that the contract for this procurement will require a fixed price, meaning that the seller guarantees the price and it will not change.

Sophie also develops the criteria that will be used to select the winning proposal. Deco Productions is known for the reliability of its products, so she sets quality as the highest requirement. Though not as important as quality, her project has a fairly tight budget, so the cost of the demo is set as the second criteria. Sophie has always found that a seller's reputation is important, so she makes this the third factor. This results in the following criteria:

- Professional quality   50%
- Cost (fixed price)   30%
- Seller reputation   20%

Deco Productions has a standard legal contract template for work of this type. Sophie includes this template as an appendix. And finally, she adds the SOW as a second appendix.

Reading through the RFP and SOW documentation, she feels confident that prospective sellers will have the information they need to submit a proposal. Now, on to the next step: creating the list of prospective sellers who will receive these documents.

CHOOSING THE SELLER

During this stage of the procurement process, potential sellers are identified through activities such as:

- the Project Manager's expertise and awareness of potential sellers;
- consultation with colleagues or consultants;
- online or similar searches of potential sellers.

In addition, advertising may be placed online or in industry journals in order to make prospective sellers aware of an upcoming procurement. Government projects normally require that advertising take place in order that all potential sellers have an opportunity to participate.

Once prospective sellers are identified, the prepared RFP and SOW documents are sent to each company. It is now up to the sellers to decide whether they will respond to the procurement. From the seller's perspective, they will assess whether they have the capabilities and resources available to provide the requested work. The prospective sellers that decide to participate will create a proposal based on the requirements of the RFP and SOW.

After a period of time, the buyer should receive a number of proposals from the prospective sellers. The challenge for the buyer is to choose one of the proposals. Various methods may be used to evaluate the proposals, including:

- analysis of the proposal documents;
- discussion with the prospective sellers;
- site visits to the prospective sellers' facilities;
- presentations or demonstrations by the sellers.

Once the buyer is selected, the next activity is the creation of a contract between the buyer and the seller. For large, complex procurements, the development of a contract can be a large effort taking a significant amount of time. The information contained in the contract should include specific details regarding:

- the deliverables to be produced;
- the due dates for all deliverables;
- the price to be paid by the buyer;
- the process to report and monitor the status of the work;
- the process to accept the deliverables;
- the process to manage changes to the required work;
- the process to resolve disagreements.

The importance of the contract cannot be overstated as it defines all aspects of the work to be completed by the seller and all obligations each party has to the other. Any disagreements that occur during the course of the procurement will be resolved according to the wording of the contract. Once both parties sign the contract, the work of the procurement may begin.

Case Study Update: Choosing the Seller

Sophie puts the finishing touches on the Statement of Work document and saves it on her laptop. Now that she has completed the documentation of the procurement requirements, her mind turns to the challenge of finding an organization to complete the work.

It is very important to take care when selecting a seller, as whatever they accomplish during the project will reflect (either positively or negatively) on the project team and Deco Productions. Sophie knows from experience that customers will hold her accountable for the quality of the final product regardless of who actually performed the work.

From personal experience, Sophie knows of one company that could perform the job. After making phone calls to her colleagues, she adds two more companies to the list. And finally, after an online search, she finds a few more companies that look promising. After locating the addresses of each of the potential sellers, Sophie sends the RFP and SOW to each company. They now have until the due date defined in the RFP to reply with a proposal.

As the April 10th deadline approaches, a number of proposals arrive. Sophie looks through the options and weighs the pros and cons of each. After a period of time, she picks her top three proposals, from CityScape Inc., Designview Video, and TDR Online.

In preparation for the selection of the winning proposal, Sophie organizes an evaluation committee consisting of Arun (the Project Sponsor), Jason (the Business Analyst), and herself. Sophie also calls each of the references provided in the proposals. Sophie knows that it's easy to "talk a good game" in a proposal, but a satisfied customer who is willing to be used as a reference is a much greater indicator of future success.

Glancing at her watch and realizing it's time for the evaluation meeting, Sophie gathers the proposals and heads to the meeting room. Sophie writes the evaluation criteria previously developed (professional quality, cost, and seller reputation) on a flip chart. She then goes around the table asking each person to provide a ranking from 1 to 10 for each. Once the ranking is complete and the results are compiled into a spreadsheet, Designview Video emerges as the clear winner.

Following the meeting, Sophie contacts Designview Video to inform them that they have been selected for the project. During the discussion, she indicates that she'll send the contract to them shortly. Over the next few days, both parties make a number of adjustments to the contract. After a final review, both parties sign the contract and the work is now ready to begin.

The following is the spreadsheet that was used to evaluate the three sellers. The assessment of each seller was entered under the Score column. The Weighted Score column was then calculated (by multiplying the score times the weight). This generates a total weighted score for each seller.

Evaluation of Seller Proposals

Project		DCV4Launch–DecoCam V4 Product Launch					
		CityScape Inc.		Designview Video		TDR Online	
Criteria	Weight	Score	Weighted Score	Score	Weighted Score	Score	Weighted Score
Professional Quality	50%	8	4.0	8	4.0	6	3.0
Cost	30%	6	1.8	9	2.7	5	1.5
Seller Reputation	20%	7	1.4	9	1.8	9	1.8
Total			7.2		8.5		6.3

MONITORING THE SELLER'S PERFORMANCE

Now that the seller has been selected and the contract has been signed, the seller may begin to perform the work of the procurement. It is very important to have a detailed and accurate contract as it guides the seller and defines what will be performed for the project.

While the buyer is not producing the deliverables, they still have a significant role during this stage of the procurement. There are three main activities to be performed:

1. Monitoring the progress of the procurement work.
2. Verifying the deliverables.
3. Managing issues and changes.

A regular status reporting process should be defined in the contract indicating how the seller reports their progress to the buyer on a regular basis. This may include regular status meetings, status reports, visits to the seller's facilities, and demonstrations of the work-in-progress. For most projects, there will also be work performed internally, so the status report created by the seller will be added or merged with the overall project status information.

As the work is being performed, the buyer will be involved in verifying that the deliverables meet the quality levels defined in the contract. This may be a formal quality control process or involve a simpler inspection of the deliverables.

Issues and changes are almost certain to occur during a project procurement. Similar to internal project work, processes should be established to manage the resolution of issues and the management of change. Changes that occur during a procurement often require the contract to be updated, which may then impact other contract provisions such as extending the delivery date or increasing the price.

Throughout the project, disagreements between the buyer and seller often occur and are normally handled through ongoing communication and negotiation. In some instances, disagreements may occur that cannot be resolved through negotiation. In these cases, legal remedies will be required. Depending on the disagreement, the buyer and seller could agree to mediation (where an external mediator facilitates a non-binding agreement) or arbitration (where an external arbitrator creates a binding agreement). The ultimate resolution is litigation, which occurs if the buyer or seller sues the other party.

Once all work is complete as defined by the terms in the contract, final payments are made and the contract is closed.

CHAPTER SUMMARY

Key Concepts

1. A Make or Buy Analysis should be used to determine whether the work of a project should be produced internally by the project team (Make) or by an external organization (Buy).
2. In order to communicate the requirements of a procurement, a Request for Proposal (RFP) and Statement of Work (SOW) should be produced and sent to prospective sellers.
3. Proposals sent by prospective sellers should be evaluated in order to select a seller.
4. A contract should be negotiated which will govern all work to be completed during the procurement.
5. Once the work defined by the contract is underway, the buyer should monitor the seller's performance.
6. When the work of the seller is completed and approved by the buyer, the contract is closed, ending the procurement.

Key Terminology

Buyer: The organization that purchases the product, service, or result from another organization.

Contract: A legal agreement between the buyer and seller that documents the content and conditions of the procurement.

Make or Buy Analysis: The process of comparing the creation of products, services, or results within the project to their creation by another organization.

Request for Proposal: A document that describes the characteristics of a procurement to enable prospective sellers to submit proposals to the buyer.

Seller: The organization that produces the product, service, or result for sale to another organization.

Statement of Work: A description of the product, services, or results to be provided during a project.

DISCUSSION QUESTIONS

1. Given recent business trends, do you think that companies will increase or decrease their procurement activities? Explain your reasoning.

2. Does the procurement process increase or decrease the amount of planning and documentation required for a project that may otherwise have been completed internally?

3. Does the presence of a legal contract change the way the project is managed?

4. Perform an online search to research problems that occur during project procurement. Summarize five common problems that may occur.

16 Closing the Project

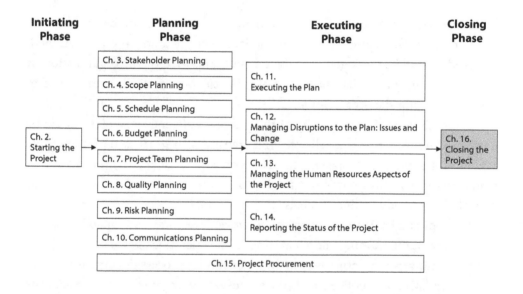

Initiating Phase	Planning Phase	Executing Phase	Closing Phase

Planning Phase:
- Ch. 3. Stakeholder Planning
- Ch. 4. Scope Planning
- Ch. 5. Schedule Planning
- Ch. 6. Budget Planning
- Ch. 7. Project Team Planning
- Ch. 8. Quality Planning
- Ch. 9. Risk Planning
- Ch. 10. Communications Planning

Initiating Phase:
- Ch. 2. Starting the Project

Executing Phase:
- Ch. 11. Executing the Plan
- Ch. 12. Managing Disruptions to the Plan: Issues and Change
- Ch. 13. Managing the Human Resources Aspects of the Project
- Ch. 14. Reporting the Status of the Project

Closing Phase:
- Ch. 16. Closing the Project

Ch. 15. Project Procurement

INTRODUCTION TO CLOSING THE PROJECT

Once all of the deliverables of the project are created and all activities are executed, the Executing Phase ends. The project now enters the fourth and final phase of the project, the Closing Phase.

While the Closing Phase is very important, it often receives insufficient attention. As new projects are initiated, there is a risk that the focus will shift to the new projects at the expense of the closing activities of an existing project. This tendency should be avoided and the following closing activities should take place:

- Transitioning the output of the project to the operations of the organization
- Reporting the results of the project
- Storing the project documents and files
- Documenting the lessons learned

TRANSITIONING TO THE OPERATIONS OF THE ORGANIZATION

Most projects create output that will remain in the organization beyond the end of the project. For example, while the project to create a new product will end, the product will be marketed, distributed, and supported by the organization. It is therefore imperative that the output of the project is effectively transitioned to the operations of the organization.

Depending on the complexity of the project's deliverables, a plan should be developed in order to ensure the effective transition. A great deal of knowledge regarding the project's scope should have been gained during the project, and it is important that this knowledge isn't lost once the project ends. Therefore, this plan should consider actions such as:

- providing a demonstration of the project's features and capabilities;
- providing training and mentoring to the operations personnel;
- creating or updating user manuals or similar process documents;
- updating the policies and procedures of the organization to reflect the changes that resulted from the project;
- transferring project personnel to the operations area (either on a temporary or permanent basis).

Case Study Update: Transitioning to the Operations of the Organization

The May 8th deadline to complete the project's deliverables has arrived and Sophie is happy to report to Arun that the product launch is ready. While it was a great deal of work and there were more than a few tense moments, it all came together in the end.

Sophie knows, though, that this is not the end of the project. She remembers a project from a couple of years ago when she didn't pay enough attention to the closing activities and instead shifted her focus to a new initiative. The resulting problems were enormous—the operations personnel at Deco Productions struggled to understand and support the new product without her guidance. Not only did this detract from the success of her project, but it also caused some damage to her relationship with the operations managers. Chalking it up to inexperience, she resolved to never ignore the closing activities again.

Checking the project schedule, she sees that three days of closing activities are planned. Her first priority is to ensure that the Marketing department has all the information they need to effectively support this product launch. Pulling out her notepad, she jots down the following activities:

- Schedule a demonstration of the trade show products (e.g., the banners, holographic cards, multimedia demo).
- Schedule a presentation of the promotional video to the Project Sponsor and key stakeholders.
- Update the Marketing department's documentation to reorder banner stands, holographic cards, murals, and tripods.

Given these activities, she's confident that the Marketing department will have everything it needs to successfully market the product.

REPORTING THE RESULTS OF THE PROJECT

At the end of the project, it is useful to remember that the project was initiated based on the anticipated costs and benefits. The Business Case and Project Charter, created during the Initiating Phase, contain this information.

The question that must be answered is whether the project achieved the costs and benefits that were originally documented. Accurately answering this question is important as it may cause changes in processes for future projects. For example, if a project was unsuccessful, this may prompt a review of how the project was managed. The determination of the project results may also cause changes in compensation (e.g., project bonuses, salary raises) or promotions depending on the success of the project.

The results of the project are documented in a **Final Project Report**. This report should measure whether the project achieved its objectives and give a detailed report regarding its scope, budget, and schedule performance. The Final Project Report will be distributed to the Project Sponsor and other key stakeholders.

Depending on the objectives of the project, research may be required in order to gather the feedback of project stakeholders or measure the performance of the project. One of the challenges of this measurement is that the objectives of projects often include performance measures that may only become known in the future (e.g., within the next quarter or next year).

In addition to the creation of the Final Project Report, a final review meeting is often scheduled with the Project Sponsor and other key stakeholders. The agenda for the meeting would normally follow the outline of the final report and would demonstrate the results and performance of the project.

The Final Project Report template is as follows:

Final Project Report Template

FINAL PROJECT REPORT	
Project Name	[This section contains the project name that should appear consistently on all project documents. Organizations often have project naming conventions.]
Date Produced	[Date the Final Project Report is produced.]
Project Sponsor	[Name of Project Sponsor.]
Project Manager	[Name of Project Manager.]
Project Goals	
Project Charter	[The project goals from the Project Charter.]
Actual Results	[The actual results achieved for each of the project goals from the Project Charter.]
Project Objectives	
Project Charter	[The project objectives from the Project Charter.]
Actual Results	[The actual results achieved for each of the project objectives from the Project Charter.]
Completion Date	
Project Charter	[The target date from the Project Charter.]
Actual Results	[The actual date(s) achieved for each of the target date(s) from the Project Charter.]
Budget	
Project Charter	[The budget from the Project Charter plus approved budget changes made during the project.]
Actual Results	[The actual costs incurred for the project.]

Case Study Update: Reporting the Results of the Project

Checking the Communication Management Plan, Sophie sees that the Final Project Meeting is scheduled for May 13th. The Final Project Report will be reviewed at this meeting, so it's time to get started on this document. The CEO, Casey Serrador, who is known for asking very detailed questions, will attend this meeting. It will be important to thoroughly prepare beforehand.

Overall, the project performed extremely well. All of the project goals and objectives were met. While the project's final cost of $61,250 did exceed the original budget of $60,000, there were two approved project changes that added $2,000 to the project budget, and the decision to outsource the Multimedia Demo added $600 to the budget. Therefore, Sophie was actually $1,350 under budget for the project. This reminds her of the importance of an effective change management process. Without the documentation of the approved changes, she might have found herself explaining why she was over budget.

As she completes the Final Project Report, she's feeling very good about the results of the project. After sending a copy of the report to Casey and Arun, she also sends a copy to the project team with a note of thanks for another terrific effort on their part.

The Final Project Report produced for the case study project is as follows:

Final Project Report

FINAL PROJECT REPORT	
Project Name	DCV4Launch–DecoCam V4 Product Launch
Date Produced	May 13, 2020
Project Sponsor	Arun Singh
Project Manager	Sophie Featherstone
Project Goals	
Project Charter	The goals of the project are to successfully launch DecoCam V4 by the project target dates, within the project budget, and to support the company's goal of a 5% increase in DecoCam's market share.
Actual Results	Target Dates: The project met the target dates (see below for details). Budget: The final project cost was within the updated project budget (see below for details). Market Share: As all objectives were completed, this project supported the company's goals of a 5% increase in market share. The assessment of the market share achieved will become known in the next six months.

Continued

Project Objectives	
Project Charter	The objectives of the project are to: • Update the product information on the company website and printed materials. • Promote the new product through existing communication channels. • Create a promotional video. • Create trade show materials.
Actual Results	All of the project objectives were achieved.
Completion Date	
Project Charter	May 8, 2020 (product launch) May 13, 2020 (project complete)
Actual Results	The project is ready to launch by May 7, 2020 (one day early). The project will be closed on May 13, 2020.
Budget	
Project Charter	$60,000
Actual Results	The final costs for the project were $61,250. The original Project Charter budget was increased to $62,600 during the project due to the following approved changes: • Change the trade show giveaways to resemble a picture frame rather than a postcard ($400). • Upgrade the software required to create the Multimedia Demo ($1,600). • Outsource the development of the Multimedia Demo ($600). Based on the modified budget, the project was under budget by $1,350.

STORING THE PROJECT DOCUMENTS AND FILES

During the project, a number of project documents are created. This includes project management documents, such as the Project Charter, Project Scope Statement, and Project Status Reports. Retention of these documents is useful for future teams, as it can be helpful to review the plans and progress of past projects.

The Project Documentation Guidelines that were creating during the communications planning outline the storage location for the project documents. During the Closing Phase, the Project Manager should ensure that all project documents are stored as required.

Additionally, a number of files are created during projects, such as spreadsheets, graphics files, software files, etc. These files may be needed for future projects and for the operations area of the company in order to provide ongoing support. The Project Manager should also ensure that all of the project files are stored as required.

Case Study Update: Storing the Project Documents and Files

Without a doubt, one of Sophie's least favourite closing activities is locating and storing all of the project documents and files. Inevitably, despite her careful creation of the Project Documentation Guidelines, many of the documents and files are scattered in various locations.

However, she knows that it is an important activity to complete. During the DecoCam project, she reviewed the project documents from a previous product launch project on a number of occasions. This information was only available to her because a Project Manager from a previous project stored the documents and files at the end of the project. With this in mind, she starts moving documents and files into the appropriate folders.

DOCUMENTING THE LESSONS LEARNED

While each project is unique, many project processes are repeated. Taking the opportunity to review these processes, identify improvements, and document what was learned is key to the improvement of project performance. This also promotes the spread of project-based learning within the organization.

Collecting and documenting the lessons learned should involve as many project team members and other stakeholders as possible. Often the discussion of a problem encountered will generate ideas for potential improvements on future projects.

Care should be taken that this process does not become a discussion of performance problems or an opportunity to assign blame. Issues related to individual performance should not be raised during this meeting. When holding a Lessons Learned Meeting, the ground rules for the meeting should be discussed beforehand.

The following is the **Lessons Learned Report** template:

Lessons Learned Report Template

LESSONS LEARNED REPORT	
Project Name	[This section contains the project name that should appear consistently on all project documents. Organizations often have project naming conventions.]
Project Sponsor	[Name of Project Sponsor.]
Project Manager	[Name of Project Manager.]

Continued

What went well during the project?
[List something that went well or was successful during the project.]

What did not go well during the project?
[List something that did not go well or was unsuccessful during the project.]

What should we do differently next time?	How will this be done?
[List ideas for process improvements for future projects.]	[Provide detail about how the process improvement could be performed or achieved.]

Case Study Update: Documenting the Lessons Learned

At the end of each project, Sophie schedules a meeting in order to gather feedback from those involved in the project. She invites the project team, the Project Sponsor (Arun), and the Resource Manager (Adrian Binkley) to her meeting.

First, she asks each person to brainstorm on the following questions:

- What went well during the project?
- What did not go well during the project?
- What could be improved upon for the next project?

Sophie gives each person a stack of sticky notes and asks them to write down one idea per sticky note. Next, she asks them to stick the notes on the wall, with the "went well" notes on the left, the "did not go well" notes in the centre, and the "could be improved" notes on the right.

As Sophie facilitates the discussion, she groups similar notes together, as multiple people will often come up with the same or similar ideas. She discusses each idea with the group in order to ensure that she understands it fully and that she gathers all of the important information. Once the discussion is complete, she records the results of the meeting in a Lessons Learned Report.

Sophie finds that this process helps her effectively manage the meeting so that each person is able to provide input and it is less likely that anyone will be able to dominate the discussion.

The following is the Lessons Learned Report created for the project:

Lessons Learned Report

LESSONS LEARNED REPORT	
Project Name	DCV4Launch–DecoCam V4 Product Launch
Project Sponsor	Arun Singh
Project Manager	Sophie Featherstone

What went well during the project?

The project kickoff meeting was very effective. The stakeholders found that it was very informative and they were able to understand the objectives of the project.

The Project Scope Statement contained a useful level of detail and team members found that it was helpful as they completed their tasks during the project.

The duration estimates for the project's activities were accurate. Most activities were completed in the planned duration.

The on-the-job training provided by Maddy to Eli seemed to work well.

The level of risk management seemed to be effective. There were no significant surprises during the project.

What did not go well during the project?

Teams members were not quite sure when their tasks were scheduled. While this information was contained in the project management software, they did not have access to it and were often unsure about the schedule.

The cost estimates for materials seemed to be optimistic—when they were purchased, the prices tended to be higher than estimated. The sales tax also didn't seem to be included in the original estimates.

The team members were not always available when originally planned in the Project HR Requirements spreadsheet. This necessitated that the project schedule be updated numerous times.

There were times during the project when there wasn't enough communication between project team members. This caused problems regarding the project's quality that needed to be addressed later in the project.

A number of problems regarding the project's quality came up at the end of the project. A great deal of work took place to correct the issues.

What should we do differently next time?	How will this be done?
Ensure team members know what their tasks are for each week.	Investigate ways to produce individual weekly task reports for each team member. This will ensure each team member is aware of their tasks.
Improve cost estimating.	Spend additional time validating the material resources estimates through online checks of the supplier websites. Be sure to include the sales tax in the estimate and assume an additional 10% cost to account for possible price increases.

Continued

Improve resource estimating and management.	Plan a bi-weekly meeting between the Project Manager and the Resource Manager to ensure the Project HR Requirements spreadsheet remains accurate.
Improve the communication within the project team.	In future projects, ensure that all team members understand that the daily huddle is a mandatory meeting.
Put more focus on project quality.	Once the Quality Assurance Plan is created, hold a team meeting to review the document and provide feedback.

Case Study Update: Epilogue

Arun Singh settles into his seat at the Consumer Electronics Show in Las Vegas, Nevada. Casey Serrador, the CEO of Deco Productions, is the keynote speaker. While he awaits Casey's introduction, he thinks about the recently completed DecoCam V4 project. As the Project Sponsor, he is pleased that the product launch was successful. The articles and blog reviews have been extremely positive. Activity on the company's social media channels has increased significantly and the promotional video has been viewed over 100,000 times.

After Casey's presentation, Arun walks over the trade show area. On his way, he waves to Sophie, Chris, and Maddy, who are on their way to another presentation. As he walks up to the Deco Productions booth, he notices a number of things. The DecoCam signs are very noticeable and are attracting many of the conference attendees, who seem to like the holographic picture frames—a few are even asking if they can have one or two more. There are also small lineups forming to view the Multimedia Demo. Arun makes a mental note to order a least two more cameras and tripods for the next conference. At that moment, Casey walks up to him.

"Hello Arun! Your launch of DecoCam was just great. Thank you for getting this done."

"Thanks Casey. But I couldn't have done it without Sophie and her fantastic team. They really did some great work."

Smiling, Casey replies, "Well, that's good. Version 5 of DecoCam is already on the drawing board, so your team will have a new product to launch soon!"

CHAPTER SUMMARY

Key Concepts

1. The product, service, or results of the project should be transferred to the operations of the organization.
2. The results of the project should be summarized and reported.
3. All project-related documentation should be archived for possible future reference.
4. The project's performance should be reviewed in order to document the lessons learned for future projects.

Key Terminology

Final Project Report: A closing document that contains a summary of the results of the project.

Lessons Learned Report: A closing document that summarizes the experiences of a project, including what went well, what did not go well, and what should be done differently for the next project.

DISCUSSION QUESTIONS

1. Why is it important to transfer the output of the project to the operations area of the company? What could happen if this step wasn't performed effectively?
2. Often the results of a project will not be known until a future date, sometimes long after a project has been completed. For example, if one of the product's goals was to increase the market share of a product, this objective cannot be determined until at least six months or more following the completion of the project. What effect does this have on the Final Project Report?
3. Conducting a Lessons Learned Meeting can be challenging, as team members may feel they are being criticized for mistakes they may have made. How can you run the meeting so that it does not focus on individual performance?
4. Perform an online search to research project closing checklists. Describe any other activities that may take place during closing that were not mentioned in this chapter.

PART V

AGILE PROJECT MANAGEMENT

Up to this point in this text, the focus has been on the traditional tools and techniques of project management. For many projects, the process of developing a plan and then executing the plan is an effective project management approach. This is especially true for projects in which the requirements are well-understood and not likely to change significantly, the technology used is relatively stable, or the duration of the project is relatively short. Additionally, projects involving construction, events, or project procurement are well-suited to this approach, as well as any projects that require the coordination of high-cost equipment or materials.

Conversely, there are many other types of projects where this approach may not be as effective. Some project scopes, particularly those related to software and technology, are often difficult to define prior to execution, due to changing consumer tastes, market conditions, or advances in technology. For these projects, problems often occur when the customer is expected to finalize their requirements in advance and then wait an extended period of time in order to receive the results. Often by the time the project is completed, the product received by the customer no longer meets their needs.

To address these situations, a number of different development methodologies have been developed, such as Scrum and Kanban. These methodologies and others have collectively become known as Agile methodologies. The use of Agile project management has greater potential for managing projects in an environment of uncertainty and continual change. Agile project management is an iterative and incremental methodology—instead of attempting to minimize or manage change, it expects and embraces change.

The following unit will focus on the Scrum framework as it demonstrates many of the concepts of Agile project management.

17 An Overview of Agile Project Management

INTRODUCTION TO AGILE PROJECT MANAGEMENT

In order to demonstrate the concepts of Agile project management, the case study project will be reset to its starting point. However, this time it will be performed using the **Scrum** framework rather than traditional project management.

THE SCRUM PROCESS

During Scrum, a number of iterations known as **Sprints** are performed by the **Scrum Team**. Each Sprint is relatively brief, usually lasting one to four weeks. During each Sprint, the following takes place:
- Sprint planning
- Development work
- Daily Stand-up Meeting
- Sprint Review
- Sprint Retrospective[1]

Each Sprint should be the same length. For example, a project should not schedule a two-week Sprint followed by a four-week Sprint. A consistent Sprint duration creates a rhythm for the project that can be productive for the team.

Once a Sprint is complete, another immediately begins. This process continues until the project work is complete and the project closes.

PROJECT INITIATION

The DecoCam V4 Product Launch project is initiated using the same processes as traditional project management. The Business Case and Project Charter documents provide the goals and objectives necessary for the project team to perform effectively.

Case Study Update: Project Initiation

Sophie has recently been appointed to be the Scrum Master for the DecoCam V4 Product Launch project. She reviews the completed Business Case and Project Charter documents. By all estimates, it looks like the product will be very successful once it's completed. Arun Singh is the Project Sponsor for this project and she's looking forward to working with him again.

As the project will be performed using the Scrum framework, Sophie and Arun meet to map out the high-level direction of the project. Due to the short timeframe of the project, one-week Sprints will be performed. This will provide very timely feedback to the Sprint Team as they develop the product launch.

As Sophie leaves the meeting, she shifts her focus to her next priority: putting together the Scrum Team.

THE SCRUM TEAM

The three roles that make up the Scrum team are the **Product Owner, Development Team,** and **Scrum Master.**

Product Owner

The Product Owner is the voice of the customer and represents the stakeholders of the project. The Product Owner has the responsibility of managing a prioritized list of items that may be implemented during the project. This list is known as the **Product Backlog.**

The Product Owner works with the Scrum Team to ensure that they understand the items contained in the Product Backlog and their priority level. The Product Owner also helps the Scrum Team to understand the business context for the Product Backlog items and interacts with other project stakeholders as necessary to address outstanding issues.

Although the Project Owner is a single person on the team, they may represent the views of a number of individual stakeholders or a committee. Only the Product Owner may change the Product Backlog.

Development Team

The Development Team is responsible for completing the work of each Sprint. It is a self-directed, cross-functional team that completes all aspects of the development work.

While individuals may have specific skill sets, the Development Team does not have sub-teams based on specialized skills (e.g., a programming team or a testing team). It is expected that each team member performs various functions as required during the Sprint, with accountability for the work residing with the Development Team as a whole.

Scrum Master

The Scrum Master is responsible for ensuring Scrum processes are understood and followed. They do not directly manage the work performed by the Development Team. Instead, the Scrum Master provides advice and coaching as required and works to remove obstacles to the Development Team's progress. They ensure that the sequence of meetings take place according to the Scrum framework and will interact with the project stakeholders as needed. The Scrum Master serves the needs of the project rather than directing its activities.

Case Study Update: The Scrum Team

In addition to Sophie (Scrum Master), Jason Brown is assigned to this project as the Product Owner. The Development Team is assigned to this project as follows:

- Chris Sandburg (graphic design)
- Sarah Pierce (communications)
- Maddy Wen (marketing)
- Eli Briggs (videography)

While each of the Development Team members possess specific skills (as indicated above), during the project they are known as Developers. They are expected to perform the work as required, from both within and outside their own specialties. This requires communication, cross training, and mentoring within the Development Team.

Now that the team is in place, the first Sprint is ready to begin.

SPRINT PLANNING

The first meeting of a Sprint is called the Sprint Planning Meeting and is attended by the Scrum Team. The length of this meeting will vary depending on the duration of the Sprint. As a guideline, a four-hour Sprint Planning Meeting would be appropriate for a two-week Sprint.

At the meeting, the items contained in the Product Backlog are reviewed and considered for possible inclusion in the Sprint, based on the priorities provided by the Product Owner. The primary questions to be resolved are:

1. What Product Backlog items can be accomplished during the Sprint?
2. How will the work be performed in order to deliver these items during the Sprint?

The Development Team provides the answers to these questions. The Product Owner's role is to advise the team regarding the priority of the Product Backlog items and to provide the business context. The Scrum Master ensures the Scrum process is followed and provides coaching to the Scrum Team members as needed.

The items that will be accomplished in the Sprint are listed in the **Sprint Backlog** and this becomes the **Sprint Goal**. This goal represents the Scrum Team's commitment for the Sprint. The implementation of the items in the Sprint Backlog creates the **Product Increment,** which is the updated version of whatever is being produced by the project. A Product Increment is not a "work-in-progress" deliverable. Instead, it is a tested, working version of the product that could be released to the customer.

Case Study Update: Sprint Planning

It's 8:30 a.m. on Monday morning and the **Sprint Planning Meeting** is ready to begin. The meeting is scheduled for the next two hours and everyone is looking forward to getting the project up and running. In addition to Sophie, the Product Owner (Jason) and the Development Team (Chris, Sarah, Maddy, and Eli) are in attendance.

The meeting begins with Jason describing each item contained in the Product Backlog. The backlog, in priority order, contains one or more items related to each of the following:

1. Press Release
2. Trade Show Signage
3. Website Updates

4. Social Media
5. Promotional Video
6. Multimedia Demo
7. Media Outreach
8. Booth Giveaways

As Jason describes each item, the Development Team asks a number of clarifying questions. Once the Product Backlog is understood, the Development Team tackles the question of what can be accomplished during the Sprint. While the priority of the items will be a primary consideration, the Development Team will also take into account other factors, including the following:

- Dependencies that may be present between the items. For example, the Press Release is the highest priority, but it may be beneficial to include it in a later Sprint in case the content of the Press Release is affected by the work of this or other Sprints.
- Items with higher complexity may need to start in an earlier Sprint. For example, the Promotional Video will likely benefit from being developed over multiple Sprints.

After a period of discussion, the Development Team selects the items that will be completed during this Sprint. This is always a challenging part of the meeting. The Development Team wants to complete as much as possible during the Sprint. However, they don't want to overcommit and not be able to deliver the items by the end of the Sprint. After extensive deliberation, the Sprint Backlog is created, resulting in the Sprint Goal.

Next, the Development Team discusses how the work will be performed during the Sprint. A number of diagrams are sketched onto a whiteboard demonstrating various scenarios that might occur. Names are written under various tasks and priorities as the team considers the challenge in front of them.

Throughout this process, Sophie keeps everything moving forward so that the Scrum Team completes the Sprint Planning process. She's careful not to direct the Development Team to include certain items or plan their work in a certain way. Her role is to facilitate, not to direct.

SPRINT DEVELOPMENT WORK

The majority of the Sprint consists of development work. Each of the Product Backlog items contained in Sprint Backlog will be developed according to the plan created during the Sprint Planning Meeting and the ongoing discussion and coordination of the Development Team.

The work performed is completely self-directed by the Development Team. The Product Owner and Scrum Master do not assign work to the Development Team or direct them on how to complete the work. The Development Team, as a whole, is responsible for the completion of the work.

The progress of the Sprint is displayed on a **Scrum Board**. This board is relatively simple, containing three columns: To-Do, Doing, and Done. Each item from the Product Backlog is represented by a sticky note and is placed in the appropriate column. At the start of the Sprint, all items are placed in the To-Do column. As work gets underway, members of the Development Team will move the appropriate sticky note items into the Doing column. When an item is completed, it is moved to the Done column. Note that moving an item to the Done column indicates that it is one hundred percent complete with no further testing or verification required.

Case Study Update: Sprint Development Work

It's 10:30 a.m. and the Sprint Planning Meeting has just completed. This leaves about four and a half days to complete the Product Backlog items that were selected. Chris heads over to the Scrum Board and writes the name of each item to be completed on a separate sticky note. He places each sticky note under the To-Do column.

Now the Development team begins its work. Frequent discussions take place during the day as different approaches are contemplated, and the work tends to pass back and forth frequently between the Developers.

As the days pass, sticky notes are moved from the To-Do column to the Doing column. A small celebration usually takes place when a sticky note moves to the Done column. The visible reminder of progress provided by the Scrum Board tends to focus and motivate the Development Team.

Jason drops by periodically during the day to answer questions and provide clarification to the Development Team. By answering questions as they come up, the momentum of the project is maintained. Sophie continues to support the team by ensuring that obstacles encountered by the Development Team are addressed and removed if possible. For example, Chris has been waiting for over 24 hours to receive an answer from the Supply Chain and Logistics department regarding the trade show banners. In order to remove this obstacle, Sophie calls the manager of the department. Within an hour, Chris receives the required information.

DAILY STAND-UP MEETING

A key element of the development work is the **Daily Stand-up Meeting**, also called the Daily Scrum. This 15-minute meeting is held at the same time on a daily basis and is attended by the Scrum Team. Each person reports:

1. What they accomplished during the last workday to accomplish the Sprint Goal.
2. What they plan to accomplish during the next workday to accomplish the Sprint Goal.
3. Any obstacles that may be blocking their work to accomplish the Sprint Goal.

The purpose of this meeting is to help coordinate the work of the Scrum Team through the exchange of progress, plans, and obstacles. However, a discussion of the project's issues and solutions does not take place during this meeting, as the 15-minute time limit does not allow for this level of detailed discussion. Further discussion of this type takes place following the meeting. The Scrum Master ensures that this process is followed.

Case Study Update: Daily Stand-up Meeting

Every morning at 8:30 a.m., Sophie meets with the Development Team for a 15-minute meeting. As the name of the meeting suggests, everyone is standing.

One by one, each Developer indicates what they accomplished in the last workday, what they plan to accomplish in the next workday, and any obstacles in their way. There are minimal questions that take place during this process. The point is to exchange information and synchronize the activities of the Development Team. However, Sophie makes special note of the obstacles as these are issues that she will help resolve following the meeting.

The meetings take place every day, at the same time, with everyone attending, no matter what is happening on the project. The Daily Stand-up Meetings are a vital aspect of the Sprint.

SPRINT REVIEW

The **Sprint Review** is a meeting held at the end of the Sprint during which the Product Increment is demonstrated. It is attended by the Scrum Team, but also may be attended by other stakeholders such as the Project Sponsor.

The Product Increment must be in a state where the product could be provided to customers if desired. This does not need to happen after each Sprint, but it should be an option.

Case Study Update: Sprint Review

It's Friday afternoon and the Sprint Review is just starting. In addition to the Scrum Team, Arun (Project Sponsor) is attending as well as Emma Mansfield (Director of Marketing). The Development Team is happy to report that all items on the Sprint Backlog were successfully completed and the Sprint Goal was met.

A member of the Development Team demonstrates the Product Increment of each completed item. This meeting included a demonstration of:

- the trade show banner file indicating the graphics and wording;
- a two-minute promotional video.

As each demonstration takes place, a number of comments and possible improvements are suggested. Upon viewing the promotional video, additional ideas are generated. Jason, the Product Owner, takes notes on the comments and suggestions, as these may be possible additions to the Product Backlog.

SPRINT RETROSPECTIVE

After the Sprint Review, the final step is to complete a **Sprint Retrospective**. This meeting is an opportunity for the Scrum Team to determine what went well, what did not go well, and what could be improved in the next Sprint.

The purpose of this retrospective is not to assign blame or assess individual performance, but to examine processes in order to make improvements for the next Sprint. The Scrum Master should be facilitating the process, but the input should come from the entire Scrum Team.

Following the completion of the Sprint Retrospective, the Scrum Master schedules the next Sprint Planning Meeting and the process repeats itself. This continues until the project work is complete and the project closes.

Case Study Update: Sprint Retrospective

Following the Sprint Review, the Scrum Team meets to perform the Sprint Retrospective. At the start of the meeting, Sophie reminds everyone that the purpose of the retrospective is to improve how the team will work together during future Sprints. The meeting is not the place to discuss Product Backlog items or specific plans for the next Sprint.

As the discussion gets underway, the team provides a number of examples regarding things that went really well. The level of collaboration was determined to be high as everyone felt that they were involved and that their point of view was being considered. The process of selecting the Product Backlog items was determined to be effective, as a reasonable yet challenging number of items was selected.

However, many team members agreed that the Daily Stand-up Meeting was a little too early. Deco Productions has a flextime policy that gives employees some flexibility to choose the start and end times of their workday. While most of the team members are in the office by 8:00 a.m., Sarah and Eli both like to arrive between 8:30 a.m. and 9:00 a.m.

Additionally, there were also a couple of quality problems where a significant error was missed by the team.

Based on the discussion, the team resolved to:

- move the Daily Stand-up Meeting one hour later to 9:30 a.m. to allow each Developer to resolve issues from the previous day before attending the meeting;
- update their quality control processes so that each Developer will ensure that their work is checked and verified by another Developer before it is considered to be Done.

As Scrum Master, Sophie takes notes on the discussion and records the recommended improvements. Both improvements will be implemented in the next Sprint.

And speaking of the next Sprint, the Sprint Planning Meeting for the second Sprint is scheduled for first thing Monday morning. Time to enjoy a well-deserved weekend to be ready for next week.

PROJECT CLOSING

Once all Sprints are complete, the project closes. The processes performed are similar to those performed during traditional project management. In particular, a Final Project Report should be produced in order to determine the success of the project. There is less need for a Lessons Learned Report during project closing as Sprint Retrospectives were completed as part of each Sprint.

Case Study Update: Project Closing

By the end of the third Sprint, all of the project objectives are complete and the Product Increment is moved to the appropriate operational areas of Deco Productions. Working with the Sprint Team, Sophie facilitates the creation of the Final Project Report. The project was very successful—the objectives were completed by the due date and it was also completed under budget.

With the completion of this project, Sophie looks forward to her next Agile project.

A COMPARISON OF TRADITIONAL AND AGILE PROJECT MANAGEMENT

There are two questions to consider when deciding whether to use Agile project management: how does it differ from traditional project management, and what is required to implement Agile project management in an organization?

While Agile project management differs from traditional methods in many ways, there are also many concepts, techniques, and skill sets that are consistent across both approaches. Implementing Agile project management in an organization goes beyond managing projects according to an Agile framework. In order to embrace this approach, there are a number of factors that need to be present in the organization.

Management Support

During traditional projects, management retains considerable control over the project. Management (represented by the Project Sponsor) must approve the content of the project and any subsequent changes. While the Project Manager may seek the input of the project team, the responsibility for the project's success rests with the Project Manager.

When using Scrum, a different approach is used which requires management support. Instead of a directive approach, self-directed project teams are given the authority to determine the work to be completed, how it will be performed, and when it is complete. The management of the organization, through the appointment of the Product Owner, provides the content and priority of the Product Backlog. However, a significant amount of control of the project primarily rests with the project team. In order for a Scrum project to function, management needs to resist actively directing the activities and decisions of the project.

Predictive vs. Adaptive Planning

During traditional projects, considerable effort is spent planning the activities and content of the project in order to create a plan that predicts the scope, time, and cost of the project accurately. The goal is to create an environment where everything goes according to the plan. The problem is that for many projects, the execution of the project turns out to be very different from what was planned. The attempt to predict the detailed schedule, scope, and budget of the project often turns out to be unsuccessful.

During Scrum, a detailed overall project plan is not created. Instead, the content of each Sprint is determined only as the Sprint is performed. The results of each Sprint influence the next Sprint. This adaptive approach allows the project to respond to new information and the conditions of the project. However, the approach does not allow the Project Manager to predict if and when certain deliverables will be delivered.

The Project Team

During traditional projects, project team members are typically added to and removed from the project as required by the project schedule. Team members may be assigned either full-time or part-time to the project, possibly working from different geographic locations.

Projects are often divided into sub-teams that are organized by skill set. As the work progresses, the in-process deliverables pass from one sub-team to the next. For example, during a systems development project, the project team is organized into three sub-teams:

- Systems analysts (responsible for designing the system)
- Developers (responsible for creating the computer programs)
- Testers (responsible for testing the computer programs)

As the project progresses, the systems analysts pass their completed design to the developers. The developers create the computer program, which is then passed to the tester who will verify the function of the completed work.

When using Scrum, the project team is dedicated full-time to the project and located in the same location. Sub-teams based on skill sets are not allowed. The teams are cross-functional, allowing team members to work on different aspects of the project.

Quality and Risk

The concepts regarding quality, whether the project is managed using Scrum or traditional project management, remain the same. That is, projects should satisfy the needs of the customer and be delivered with few failures. Quality assurance planning should take place and quality control should be performed in order to ensure the deliverables function as required. The main difference is that during an Agile project, this work takes place within each Sprint and is performed by the cross-functional team rather than by sub-teams.

Similarly, risks are almost always present and should be managed on a project, regardless of whether it is managed using Scrum or traditional methods. Risks should be identified and analyzed in each approach, with risk response and contingency planning performed as required. During Scrum, this takes place during each Sprint.

Stakeholder Communication

Stakeholders are present regardless of how the project is managed and therefore effective stakeholder management is important. Similar to the Project Manager for traditional projects, the Scrum Master often interacts with stakeholders outside the project team as required throughout the project.

The framework of the Scrum process facilitates a significant amount of communication, as follows:

- During Sprint Planning, the business needs are communicated to the Scrum Team.
- The Daily Stand-up Meetings provide a daily update of the current status of the project.
- The Scrum Board provides a visible update that can be viewed at any time by project stakeholders.
- The Sprint Review demonstrates the work completed to the stakeholders of the project.
- The repetition of Sprints throughout the project results in a constant flow of communication between the Scrum Team and the project stakeholders.

During traditional projects, the project team works separately from the project stakeholders. Therefore, communication is not inherent in the process, but instead communications are planned using the Communication Management

Plan. For example, without the Daily Stand-up Meeting, Scrum Board, and Sprint Review, traditional project management teams require regular status reports to communicate the status of the project to their stakeholders.

Project Procurement

In general, projects that involve the procurement of goods and services from other organizations are more suited to traditional project management. In many cases, in order to agree to a contract, the necessary details contained in the contract would only be available through the type of planning that takes place during traditional projects.

It is possible to perform a procurement process using Scrum; however, the contract would have to be structured to support this framework. For example, the contract could be written to specify that a certain number of Sprints are to be performed, without specifying that deliverables are to be required by a certain date.

Traditional vs. Agile Management—A Summary

Choosing a project management approach does not need to be an all or nothing decision where either Agile or traditional methods must be used exclusively. Organizations may develop blends of the two approaches as required to suit their needs and project environment.

For example, an organization could prefer to use traditional project management methods but could alter their approaches to incorporate changes, such as:
- dedicated project teams that are located at the same location to enhance teamwork and communication;
- more frequent demonstrations of project deliverables to gather additional feedback;
- breaking the project execution down into smaller intervals.

Ultimately, when managing a project, the purpose is to satisfy the customer. Depending on the project, this may be accomplished through the use of traditional project management, Agile project management, or a combination of both approaches.

CHAPTER SUMMARY

Key Concepts

1. Agile project management consists of the repetition of fixed time periods that are known as Sprints.
2. The three key roles that make up the Scrum Team are the Product Owner, Development Team, and Scrum Master.
3. During Sprint Planning, the items from the Product Backlog are selected for the Sprint and a plan is developed to complete the work.
4. During Development, the work is completed. Daily Stand-up Meetings take place at the same time each day for no more than 15 minutes.
5. During the Sprint Review, the finished product of the Sprint is demonstrated to the project stakeholders.
6. During the Sprint Retrospective, the process of the Sprint is reviewed in order to determine possible improvements.
7. During projects managed using traditional project management, the control of the project rests primarily with the Project Manager and Project Sponsor. When using Agile project management, an increased amount of control rests with the Development Team.
8. Traditional project management is predictive. The goal during planning is to determine the scope, schedule, and budget for the entire project. Agile project management is adaptive. The content of each Sprint is planned in detail and each subsequent Sprint adapts to new input and information.
9. During projects managed using traditional project management, team members can be added and removed from the project as needed, can work from different locations, and can be separated into different groups based on their skill set. During Agile projects, team members are usually dedicated full-time to the project, work from the same location, and possess cross-functional skills.
10. In both traditional and Agile project management, the effective practice of quality, risk, and stakeholder management is important.
11. Traditional project management is often used to manage project procurements given the need to define the project requirements, timeline, and budget in a contract.

Key Terminology

Daily Stand-up Meeting: A daily 15-minute meeting during which the current progress of the Sprint is reviewed. Also known as a Daily Scrum.

Development Team: The team members who are responsible for completing the work of each Sprint.

Product Backlog: The list of all potential items to be developed during the project.

Product Increment: The updated version of whatever is being produced by the project. It is a tested, working version of the product that could be released to the customer.

Product Owner: The team member who is responsible for managing the Product Backlog and is considered the voice of the customer for the project.

Scrum: A framework for project management that involves the repetition of fixed time periods (Sprints) to develop the product.

Scrum Board: A physical display of the current progress of the Sprint showing the Product Backlog items that are awaiting development, in-progress, and completed.

Scrum Master: The team member who is responsible for ensuring that Scrum processes are understood and followed.

Scrum Team: The project team for Scrum projects consisting of the Development Team, Product Owner, and Scrum Master.

Sprint: A set period of time during which work is completed and demonstrated.

Sprint Backlog: The Product Backlog items selected for the current Sprint.

Sprint Goal: The completion of all items on the Sprint Backlog for the current Sprint.

Sprint Planning Meeting: A meeting at the start of the Sprint during which the items from the Product Backlog are selected and a plan for development is completed.

Sprint Retrospective: A meeting at the end of the Sprint during which the processes of the Sprint are reviewed in order to determine possible improvements.

Sprint Review: A meeting held at the end of the Sprint during which the Product Increment is demonstrated to the project stakeholders.

DISCUSSION QUESTIONS

1. How does the Scrum Master role differ from the Project Manager role?

2. The first Sprint of your Agile project is underway, and the Project Sponsor asks for a detailed timeline of all the major deliverables. How would you respond to this request?

3. Why are the Daily Stand-up Meetings an important part of the Sprint process, and why are they only 15 minutes long?

4. Why is a Sprint Retrospective completed for each Sprint? Instead, why not just perform one at the end of the project?

5. Scrum is one of a number of Agile project management frameworks. Perform an online search and provide a short description of two other Agile project management frameworks not mentioned in this chapter.

6. Describe a project that would benefit from the use of Agile project management and a project that would benefit from the use of traditional project management. What are the characteristics of each project that led to this assessment?

7. When using Agile project management, the Development Team possesses more control over the content and planning of the project compared to traditional project management approaches. What are the potential advantages and disadvantages of having the Development Team be responsible for the completion of the work?

8. When using traditional project management, team members usually perform tasks related to their specialized skills. During Agile project management, team members are cross-functional, often performing tasks outside of their skill set. Compare the two approaches.

9. For projects that involve procurement, would it be possible to use Agile project management? If yes, how would the contract be written to accommodate this framework?

NOTE

1. Jeff Sutherland, one of the inventors of the Scrum process, describes these processes in the following text: Sutherland, J. (2014). *Scrum—The Art of Doing Twice the Work in Half the Time*. Crown Business, New York, NY.

Appendix

The Case Study Project Management Documents

Business Case (see pages 18–19)

BUSINESS CASE	
Proposed Project	DecoCam V4 Product Launch
Date Produced:	March 2, 2020
Background	Deco Productions is updating its DecoCam product to include a new feature known as the Photo Assistant.
	The subject of this business case is the work involved to launch this new product.
Business Need/ Opportunity	DecoCam is currently the leading camera-related application in the mobile market and it is important that this leadership position is maintained. An effective launch of the new version of DecoCam will positively impact the sales of the new product leading to increased revenues and market share of this product.
	An important objective of this project is that it must be ready to launch once the development of the new product is complete.
Options	The following are the high-level options:
	A. Soft product launch
	• Product information would be updated on the company website and printed materials, but otherwise no additional promotional activities would take place.
	B. Moderate product launch
	• This would include Option A along with promotional activities using the company's existing communication channels.
	C. Full product launch
	• This would include Option B along with a promotional video and the creation of trade show materials.

Cost-Benefit Analysis

Option A—Soft product launch
Costs
• Budget: $10,000
• Possibility of delaying the product launch date: 1%
Benefits
• Market share: estimated that DecoCam will maintain its current market share

Option B—Moderate product launch
Costs
• Budget: $25,000
• Possibility of delaying the product launch date: 5%
Benefits
• Market share: estimated that DecoCam will increase its current market share by 3% within one year of the product launch
• Brand recognition: moderate increase in the recognition of Deco Productions as a provider of high-quality photography and video-related products

Option C—Full product launch
Costs
• Budget: $60,000
• Possibility of delaying the product launch date: 10%
Benefits:
• Market share: estimated that DecoCam will increase its current market share by 6% within one year of the product launch
• Brand recognition: significant increase in the recognition of Deco Productions as a provider of high-quality photography and video-related products

Recommendation

Given the potential for increased marketing share and brand recognition, Option C (full product launch) is recommended.

Project Charter (see page 22)

PROJECT CHARTER	
Project Name	DCV4Launch–DecoCam V4 Product Launch
Date Produced	March 25, 2020
Project Goals	The goals of the project are to successfully launch DecoCam V4 by the target date, within the project budget, and to support the company's goal of a 5% increase in DecoCam's market share.
Project Objectives	The objectives of the project are to: • Update the product information on the company website and printed materials. • Promote the new product through existing communication channels. • Create a promotional video. • Create tradeshow materials.
Project Budget	$60,000
Project Sponsor	Arun Singh, Vice-President, Mobile Products Distribution
Project Manager	Sophie Featherstone, Senior Project Manager

Additional Key Project Stakeholders

Casey Serrador, CEO, Deco Productions

Jackson Woodhouse, Vice-President, Customer Support

Brittany Bianchi, Vice-President, Product Development

Overall Project Milestones	Dates
Project starts	March 23, 2020
Project approval	March 25, 2020
Trade show materials complete	May 8, 2020
Project complete	May 13, 2020

Overall Project Risks

Errors are present in the product launch materials.

Delays during the project cause the product launch to be late.

Stakeholder Analysis (see page 31)

STAKEHOLDER ANALYSIS				
Project Name	DCV4Launch–DecoCam V4 Product Launch			
Name	**Project Role**	**Power**	**Interest**	**Level of Support**
Casey Serrador	Founder and CEO	High	High	Supportive
Arun Singh	Project Sponsor	High	High	Supportive
Other V4 Project Managers	Project Managers of the other V4 projects	High	Low	Neutral
Jackson Woodhouse	Vice-President, Customer Support	High	High	Unsupportive
Project team	Project team	Low	High	Supportive
Deco Productions employees	Employees of Deco Productions with some level of contact with the project	Low	Low	Neutral

Stakeholder Management Plan (see pages 33–34)

STAKEHOLDER MANAGEMENT PLAN		
Project Name	DCV4Launch–DecoCam V4 Product Launch	
Name	**About the Stakeholder**	**Plan**
Casey Serrador	As CEO of the company, Casey is an extremely important stakeholder. Casey is very outgoing and supportive, but she can be very demanding when it comes to the quality of her company's products and services. She does not tolerate people who are vague or evasive and she requires open and clear communication. She also promotes an open door policy that encourages employees to drop by her desk if they would like to talk to her.	• As part of this project, reports will not be provided directly to Casey, as Arun (Project Sponsor) will perform this task. • However, Casey is likely to make efforts to interact with the project team at various intervals. • Drop by her office periodically to demonstrate key aspects of the project (at least twice during the project). • Provide high-level overviews but be prepared to provide details if she requests more information. • Be open and direct with her regarding any requests for information. • Let the project team know that she may be dropping by for demos periodically.
Arun Singh	Arun is relatively new to the organization and seems concerned about creating a good first impression with this project. He is very supportive and friendly, but somewhat more reserved in nature compared to Casey's style of management. He has shown a great deal of interest in the financial aspects of the project and has expressed concern regarding the budget.	• Book informational meetings with Arun to provide him with updates and ensure that he is comfortable with the progress of the project. These can be held at increased or decreased intervals depending on his feedback. • Invite Arun to the bi-weekly team demonstration of completed deliverables. • Keep him updated regarding the budget information and alert him immediately if there is any indication that the budget will be exceeded.
Other V4 Project Managers	Many projects are interdependent, so it is important to foster positive relationships between the project teams.	• Schedule an initial meeting with each Project Manager to review their timeline and any dependencies between projects. • Respond to any requests for assistance and provide assistance when appropriate. • Send a summary of key dates to each Project Manager once the schedule is completed. Send updates to them if the key dates change during the project.

Jackson Woodhouse	Jackson has been with the organization for many years and is very loyal to the company. He has very strong convictions and is focused on providing support for Deco Productions' largest clients. In the past, he has been critical of the mobile device camera applications. He values direct discussion and likes to "tell it like it is."	• Early in the project, drop by Jackson's office to acknowledge and listen to his concerns about his preferred project option (upgraded camera software for a key customer). • Encourage his input and feedback. • During status update and reports, acknowledge the value of his department's support.
Project team	As the project team has not yet been assigned, this section cannot be completed. It is anticipated that experienced DecoCam employees will be assigned shortly.	• Keep the team well-informed by ensuring that all project documents are accessible. • Foster a positive team environment by periodically suggesting team lunches or gatherings at the end of the workday. • Check in with each team member regularly to see how their work is going and receive any feedback or concerns.
Deco Productions employees	The employees of the company are often interested in new products that are developed.	• No specific actions are planned at this time. • Answer any requests for information or updates when appropriate.

Project Requirements (see page 39)

PROJECT REQUIREMENTS	
Project Name	DCV4Launch–DecoCam V4 Product Launch

Functional Requirements

1. All DecoCam product information listed on the company website and printed materials should be updated to include Version 4 and the key characteristics of this version.
2. Promotional material should be distributed through sponsored advertisements on selected websites and through Deco Productions' social media presence.
3. A press release for this version should be created.
4. The technology blogging community should be engaged so that they cover the new release.
5. The promotional video should be professional and engaging, and should demonstrate the key features of the new version.
6. Materials should be produced for upcoming trade shows and include DecoCam signs, booth giveaways branded with the DecoCam logo, and a multimedia display that will draw trade show attendees to the booth.
7. The trade show materials should be delivered and set up at each tradeshow.

Technical/Performance Requirements

1. All promotional files and videos should be compatible with all major browsers and operating systems.
2. All files should be created in PDF format.
3. All promotional files to be accessed by customers should be under 10 MB to ensure minimal download times.

Project Scope Statement (see pages 44–45)

PROJECT SCOPE STATEMENT	
Project Name	DCV4Launch–DecoCam V4 Product Launch
Project Deliverables	

Trade Show Support	**Trade Show Signage** • The signs will be retractable banner stands. • Initial creation of five stands. • Integrate with company's existing trade show set up and branding. • Provide a visual display of the product's features. • Display information with links to more product information. • Update the trade show supplies procedures and data files to allow for the order of additional banners.
	Booth Giveaways • Consists of a flyer that resembles a postcard. • Initial creation of 2,000 postcards. • The picture side of the postcard will contain a holographic scene of an art deco building with a sign displaying the DecoCam name and logo. • The address side of the postcard will contain the necessary product and contact information. • Update the trade show supplies procedures and data files to allow for the order of additional postcards.
	Multimedia Demo • Consists of a mural showing an urban scene for visual interest. • A mobile phone will be mounted on a tripod and will run a slideshow simulating the user experience of using the DecoCam Photo Assistant feature. • Initial creation of two murals and the set up of two tripods with phones. • Update the trade show supplies procedures and data files to allow for the order of additional demo kits.
Communications	**Press Release** • Create a one-page news story following The Canadian Press style. • Distribute electronically to media on the same date that DecoCam V4 is available for download to the public.
	Media Outreach • Includes email and phone calls to encourage publicity from major online influencers (e.g., industry magazines, top technology bloggers).
	Social Media • Develop a social media strategy and calendar for the three months following the launch of the product. • Develop the content for the planned social media posts.
	Website Updates • Update the DecoCam product page to include the features of the new version. • Create an online slideshow that demonstrates the key features of the new version.

Continued

Promotions	Promotional Video
	• Develop a professional video that demonstrates how to use the new product.
	• To increase the likelihood that viewers will share the video through social media channels, the video should contain a humorous situation.
	• The message of the video will be the usefulness of the DecoCam Photo Assistant feature and how it will help average people take photos like a professional photographer.
	• The video should be no more than two minutes in length.

Project Exclusions

Distribution of social media posts. This will be performed by the marketing department.

Distribution of the DecoCam software. This will be performed by the DecoCam V4 Installation Project.

Trade show staffing and management. Documentation and supplies for the trade shows will be created and will be available for order by the marketing department.

Technical support for the website content, videos, or other materials. This will be provided by the marketing department.

Milestone-Based Schedule (see page 55)

MILESTONE	DATE
Project approved	March 25, 2020
Trade show materials complete	April 23, 2020
Communications complete	April 29, 2020
Promotional video complete	May 8, 2020
Project complete	May 13, 2020

Activity-Based Schedule (see pages 56–57)

ACTIVITY	DURATION	START DATE	END DATE
Initiating			
Initiate the project	3 days	March 23, 2020	March 25, 2020
Project approved	0 days	March 25, 2020	March 25, 2020
Planning			
Plan the project	7 days	March 26, 2020	April 3, 2020
Executing			
Trade Show Signage			
Create sign graphics/text	3 days	April 6, 2020	April 8, 2020
Order banner stands	1 day	April 9, 2020	April 9, 2020
Booth Giveaways			
Create holographic cards	2 days	April 10, 2020	April 13, 2020
Order cards	1 day	April 14, 2020	April 14, 2020
Multimedia Demo			
Create mural for booth	3 days	April 15, 2020	April 17, 2020
Develop demo slideshow	3 days	April 20, 2020	April 22, 2020
Order murals and tripods	1 day	April 23, 2020	April 23, 2020
Trade show materials complete	0 days	April 23, 2020	April 23, 2020
Social Media			
Create SM strategy	2 days	April 6, 2020	April 7, 2020
Develop SM post content	3 days	April 8, 2020	April 10, 2020
Website Updates			
Update product page	1 day	April 13, 2020	April 13, 2020
Develop online slideshow	3 days	April 14, 2020	April 16, 2020
Media Outreach			
Create outreach list	1 day	April 17, 2020	April 17, 2020
Perform outreach	5 days	April 20, 2020	April 24, 2020
Press Release			
Create press release	2 days	April 27, 2020	April 28, 2020
Send press release	1 day	April 29, 2020	April 29, 2020
Communications complete	0 days	April 29, 2020	April 29, 2020
Promotional Video			
Develop video concept	3 days	April 6, 2020	April 8, 2020
Develop video storyboard	2 days	April 9, 2020	April 10, 2020

Develop video script	5 days	April 13, 2020	April 17, 2020
Create video	15 days	April 20, 2020	May 8, 2020
Promotional video complete	0 days	May 8, 2020	May 8, 2020
Closing			
Close the project	3 days	May 11, 2020	May 13, 2020
Project complete	0 days	May 13, 2020	May 13, 2020

Activity-Based Schedule Using a Workflow Approach (see page 58)

To-Do	
Create holographic cards	Order cards
Create mural for booth	Develop demo slideshow
Order mural and tripods	Update product page
Develop online slideshow	Create outreach list
Perform outreach	Create press release
Send press release	Develop video script
Create video	Close the project

Doing	
Order banner stands	Develop SM post content
Develop video storyboard	

Done	
Initiate the Project	Plan the Project
Create sign/graphics text	Create SM strategy
Develop video concept	

Dependency-Based Schedule (Gantt Chart) (see page 59)

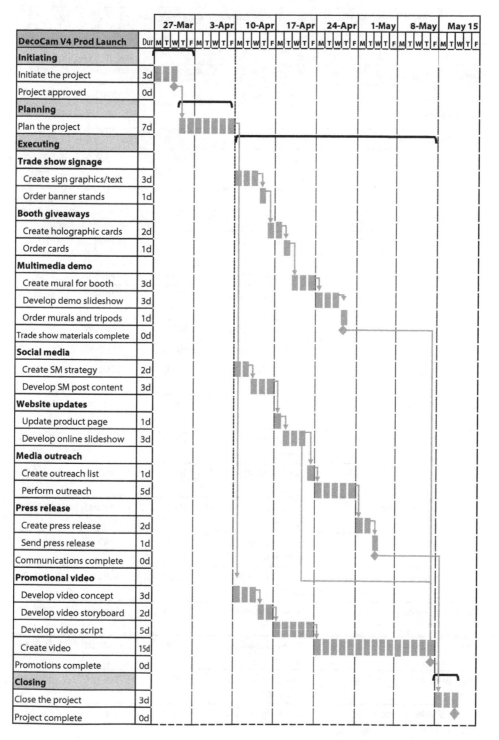

DecoCam V4 Prod Launch	Dur
Initiating	
Initiate the project	3d
Project approved	0d
Planning	
Plan the project	7d
Executing	
Trade show signage	
Create sign graphics/text	3d
Order banner stands	1d
Booth giveaways	
Create holographic cards	2d
Order cards	1d
Multimedia demo	
Create mural for booth	3d
Develop demo slideshow	3d
Order murals and tripods	1d
Trade show materials complete	0d
Social media	
Create SM strategy	2d
Develop SM post content	3d
Website updates	
Update product page	1d
Develop online slideshow	3d
Media outreach	
Create outreach list	1d
Perform outreach	5d
Press release	
Create press release	2d
Send press release	1d
Communications complete	0d
Promotional video	
Develop video concept	3d
Develop video storyboard	2d
Develop video script	5d
Create video	15d
Promotions complete	0d
Closing	
Close the project	3d
Project complete	0d

Cost Estimates (see pages 82–83)

HUMAN RESOURCES COST ESTIMATES					
Activity	**Duration (days)**	**Resource**	**% Allocated**	**Daily Rate**	**Cost**
Initiating Phase					
Initiate the project	3	Project Manager	50%	$800.00	$1,200.00
Total Initiating Phase					**$1,200.00**
Planning Phase					
Plan the project	7	Project Manager	50%	$800.00	$2,800.00
	7	Business Analyst	100%	$640.00	$4,480.00
Total Planning Phase					**$7,280.00**
Executing Phase					
Create sign graphics/ text	3	Graphic Designer	100%	$400.00	$1,200.00
Order banner stands	1	Graphic Designer	100%	$400.00	$400.00
Create holographic cards	2	Graphic Designer	100%	$400.00	$800.00
Order cards	1	Graphic Designer	100%	$400.00	$400.00
Create mural for booth	3	Graphic Designer	100%	$400.00	$1,200.00
Develop demo slideshow	3	Graphic Designer	100%	$400.00	$1,200.00
Order mural and tripods	1	Graphic Designer	100%	$400.00	$400.00
Create SM strategy	2	Communications Specialist	100%	$480.00	$960.00
Develop SM post content	3	Communications Specialist	100%	$480.00	$1,440.00
Update product page	1	Communications Specialist	100%	$480.00	$480.00
Develop online slideshow	3	Communications Specialist	100%	$480.00	$1,440.00
Create outreach list	1	Communications Specialist	100%	$480.00	$480.00
Perform outreach	5	Communications Specialist	100%	$480.00	$2,400.00
Create press release	2	Communications Specialist	100%	$480.00	$960.00
Send press release	1	Communications Specialist	100%	$480.00	$480.00
Develop video concept	3	Marketing Specialist	100%	$480.00	$1,440.00

Develop video storyboard	2	Marketing Specialist	100%	$480.00	$960.00
Develop video script	5	Marketing Specialist	100%	$480.00	$2,400.00
Create video	15	Videographer	100%	$400.00	$6,000.00
	15	Marketing Specialist	100%	$480.00	$7,200.00
Monitoring and Controlling	25	Project Manager	34%	$800.00	$6,800.00
	25	Business Analyst	20%	$640.00	$3,200.00
Total Executing Phase					**$42,240.00**
Closing Phase					
Close the project	3	Project Manager	50%	$800.00	$1,200.00
Total Closing Phase					**$1,200.00**
Total HR Cost Estimates					**$51,920.00**
Other Cost Estimates					

Item	Quantity	Description	Unit Cost	Cost
Banner stands	5	Banner stands for trades show	$200.00	$1,000.00
Holographic cards	2,000	Cards for trade show booth giveaways	$1.00	$2,000.00
Murals	2	Murals for trade show multimedia demo	$100.00	$200.00
Camera and tripod	2	Camera and tripod for trade show multimedia demo	$700.00	$1,400.00
Total Other Cost Estimates				**$4,600.00**
Total Project Cost Estimates				**$56,520.00**

Detailed Budget (Weekly) (see pages 85–86)

DETAILED BUDGET									
Project Name	DCV4Launch–DecoCam V4 Product Launch								
Cost Category	**Week ending 27-Mar**	**Week ending 3-Apr**	**Week ending 10-Apr**	**Week ending 17-Apr**	**Week ending 24-Apr**	**Week ending 1-May**	**Week ending 8-May**	**Week ending 15-May**	**Total**
Initiating									
HR costs	$1,200								$1,200
Planning									
HR costs	$2,080	$5,200							$7,280
Executing									
HR costs			$8,800	$8,800	$10,400	$7,840	$6,400		$42,240
Other costs			$1,000	$2,000	$1,600				$4,600
Closing									
HR costs								$1,200	$1,200
Total Costs	**$3,280**	**$5,200**	**$9,800**	**$10,800**	**$12,000**	**$7,840**	**$6,400**	**$1,200**	**$56,520**

Detailed Budget (Monthly) (see page 87)

DETAILED BUDGET				
Project Name		DCV4Launch–DecoCam V4 Product Launch		
Cost Category	**March**	**April**	**May**	**Total**
Initiating				
HR costs	$1,200			**$1,200**
Planning				
HR costs	$4,160	$3,120		**$7,280**
Executing				
HR costs		$34,560	$7,680	**$42,240**
Other costs		$4,600		**$4,600**
Closing				
HR costs			$1,200	**$1,200**
Total Costs	**$5,360**	**$42,280**	**$8,880**	**$56,520**

Project HR Requirements (see page 92)

PROJECT HR REQUIREMENTS								
Project Name	DCV4Launch–DecoCam V4 Product Launch							
Resource Type	**Week ending 27-Mar**	**Week ending 3-Apr**	**Week ending 10-Apr**	**Week ending 17-Apr**	**Week ending 24-Apr**	**Week ending 1-May**	**Week ending 8-May**	**Week ending 15-May**
Project Manager	2.5 days	2.5 days	1.7 days	1.7 days	1.7 days	1.7 days	1.7 days	1.5 days
Business Analyst	2 days	5 days	1 day	1 day	1 day	1 day	1 day	
Graphic Designer			5 days	5 days	4 days			
Communications Specialist			5 days	5 days	5 days	3 days		
Marketing Specialist			5 days	5 days	5 days	5 days	5 days	
Videographer			5 days	5 days	5 days	5 days	5 days	

Project Roles and Responsibilities (see pages 94–95)

PROJECT ROLES AND RESPONSIBILITIES		
Project Name	DCV4Launch–DecoCam V4 Product Launch	
Name	**Role**	**Responsibilities**
Arun Singh	Project Sponsor	• Provides funding for the project. • Provides overall direction and approves major changes for the project. • Provides final sign off for the project. • Communicates the project's progress to the senior management of Deco Productions.
Sophie Featherstone	Project Manager	• Overall responsibility for the project's completion. • Creates and maintains the project plans. • Approves minor changes and determines which changes will require Project Sponsor approval. • Manages the project team and assists each team member to resolve issues. • Communicates project updates and other information to the Project Sponsor.
Jason Brown	Business Analyst	• Completes the project scope-related documents. • Communicates project updates and any issues to the Project Manager. • Clarifies the project scope to the project team as requested. • Performs quality control for all completed deliverables.
Chris Sandburg	Graphic Designer	• Responsible for the completion of all work packages related to the trade show. • Communicates project updates and any issues to the Project Manager. • Provides graphic design consulting to the rest of the project team as required.
Sarah Pierce	Communications Specialist	• Responsible for the completion of all work packages related to media relations, social media, and updates to the website. • Communicates project updates and any issues to the Project Manager. • Provides communications consulting to the rest of the project team as required.
Maddy Wen	Marketing Specialist	• Responsible for the completion of the promotional video. • Provides direction to the Videographer. • Communicates project updates and any issues to the Project Manager. • Provides marketing consulting to the rest of the project team as required.
Eli Briggs	Videographer	• Responsible for the completion of video-related activities under the direction of the Marketing Specialist. • Communicates project updates and any issues to the Marketing Specialist.

RACI Chart (see page 96)

RACI CHART							
	Arun	**Sophie**	**Jason**	**Chris**	**Sarah**	**Maddy**	**Eli**
Trade Show Support	C	C	C	A,R	I	I	I
Communications	C	C	C	I	A,R	I	I
Promotional Video	C	C	C	I	I	A,R	R
Project Management	C	A,R	C	I	I	I	I

R-Responsible A-Accountable C-Consulted I-Informed

Project Organization Chart (see page 97)

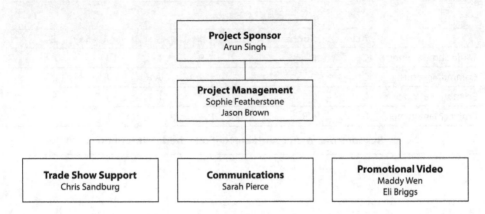

Quality Management Plan (see pages 102–103)

QUALITY MANAGEMENT PLAN	
Project Name	DCV4Launch–DecoCam V4 Product Launch
Quality Standards	

Technical Standards

1. All image files will be in the company standard file type and will meet the standard minimum resolution.
2. All video files will be in the company standard file type and will meet the standard minimum resolution.
3. All images displayed must be verified to ensure that there is no copyright infringement.

Writing Standards

1. The press release will use CP style.
2. The press release will be 250 words, with a tolerance of plus or minus 50 words.
3. All written material that will be viewed by anyone outside of the company will contain zero spelling or grammatical errors.

Social Media Standards

1. All social media content produced will meet the company's Social Media Policy in terms of content, frequency, and approved social media platforms.

Communication Standards

1. All emails must be responded to within 24 hours.
2. Meeting agendas for all formal project meetings are required 24 hours in advance of the meeting.
3. Minutes are required for all formal project meetings within 48 hours of the meeting completion.
4. The status of the project (updated schedule and budget) must be reported to the Project Sponsor on a weekly basis.

Risk List (see pages 110–111)

RISK LIST					
Project Name					
DCV4Launch–DecoCam V4 Product Launch					
#	**Risk**	**Description**	**Prob Factor**	**Impact Factor**	**Risk Score**
8	Promotional video's language translations are incorrect.	Incorrect translation of the video to French and Spanish results in customer complaints and negative publicity.	.8	8	6.4
2	Written materials contain errors.	Errors are found in the written materials such as the press release, website updates, etc.	.5	10	5.0
6	Delivery of trade show materials is delayed.	Delivery of trade show materials is delayed.	.8	5	4.0
1	Team member leaves the project.	A team member leaves the project for a prolonged period of time for any reason, such as leaving the company or illness.	.5	5	2.5
9	Social media posts attract inappropriate replies.	The social media posts created for the product launch attract inappropriate replies that result in negative publicity.	.5	5	2.5
3	Product launch is moved to an earlier date.	The release date of DecoCam V4 is moved up, necessitating an earlier product launch date.	.2	10	2.0
7	The promotional video is late.	The promotional video takes longer than expected and is not available for the product launch.	.2	8	1.6
4	New requirements are received.	New requirements are received after planning is complete, causing changes to the project's deliverables.	.5	2	1.0
10	Multimedia demo causes disorientation to customers.	The multimedia demo's virtual reality causes disorientation and dizziness to some customers.	.2	5	1.0
5	Trade show material costs are higher than expected.	When ordering the tradeshow materials (e.g., the banner stand), the actual costs are higher than originally budgeted.	.2	2	0.4

Risk Response Plan (see pages 114–116)

RISK RESPONSE PLAN				
Project Name				
DCV4Launch–DecoCam V4 Product Launch				
#	**Risk**	**Risk Response**	**Description**	**Contingency Plan**
8	Promotional video's language translations are incorrect.	Avoid	This requirement should be removed from the project due to the negative publicity that may occur if errors are made. Further work to improve the organization's translation capabilities should be performed.	The risk is avoided. No contingency plan.
2	Written materials contain errors.	Mitigate	Strict attention must be paid to the quality processes throughout the project.	Printed materials will be recalled and reproduced. The electronic material will be immediately corrected. This plan is invoked when the error is reported.
6	Delivery of trade show materials is delayed.	Mitigate	Schedule trade show materials to be delivered at least one week before they are required.	Negotiate earlier delivery date with suppliers. Inform the trade show team of the possible delay. This plan is invoked when materials are more than two days late from their original delivery date.
1	Team member leaves the project.	Mitigate	Ensure all project documentation and files are saved in the shared folder. Ensure all team members provide weekly progress updates.	Reassign work to other team members. Work with the Resource Manager to replace the missing team member as soon as possible.

Continued

				This plan is invoked when: 1. Team member is absent for more than three consecutive days. 2. Team member resigns.
9	Social media posts attract inappropriate replies.	Accept	This risk is accepted as the team cannot control the replies to social media posts.	Remove any offensive posts according to the company's social media policy. This plan is invoked when the inappropriate reply is detected. Replies to social media posts should be monitored at least twice per day.
10	Multimedia demo causes disorientation to customers.	Transfer	Create signs indicating that the demo may cause disorientation or dizziness and that people should use the demo at their own risk. Mitigate by ensuring that people must be seated when viewing the demo.	Stop the multimedia demo and provide assistance as necessary. This plan is invoked if a trade show participant displays signs of disorientation or dizziness.
3	Product launch is moved to an earlier date.	Mitigate	Activities will be scheduled to be completed as soon as possible.	Add another videographer from another area of the company. The Business Analyst will assist the other team members with their activities. This plan is invoked if the product launch date is moved.
7	The promotional video is late.	Mitigate	Weekly checkpoints are planned in order to review the progress of the video.	Add another videographer from another area of the company. This plan is invoked if the video falls behind schedule by five days or more.

| 4 | New require-ments are received. | Accept | This risk is accepted as the project scope has been planned effectively and additional requirements gathering is not recommended. | Requested changes will be assessed and either approved or rejected according to the project's change management process.

This plan is invoked when a new requirement is requested. |
| 5 | Trade show material costs are higher than expected. | Accept | This risk is accepted as the trade show material costs are a small percentage of the overall proj-ect budget. | Investigate alternate suppliers if available. Otherwise, the budget will be adjusted for the higher cost.

This plan is invoked when the trade show material costs are 10% or more over budget. |

Project Documentation Guidelines (see page 122)

PROJECT DOCUMENTATION GUIDELINES	
Project Name	DCV4Launch–DecoCam V4 Product Launch

Storage Location and Organization

All project documents will be stored on the secured project website. Sophie Featherstone will be the administrator and will grant Read or Read/Write access to the project team and certain project stakeholders as needed.

Documents will be filed in the following folders:
• Initiating
• Scope
• Schedule
• Budget
• Team/HR
• Quality
• Risk
• Communication
• Meeting Agenda and Minutes
• Status Reports
• Issues
• Changes
• Closing

Naming Conventions

All document file names will be as follows:
Project ID - Document Name - Version (if required) - Date of Report (YYYYMMDD)

Examples:
• DCV4Launch - Project Charter - 1.0 - 20200325
• DCV4Launch - Project Status Report - 20200424

Document Versions

Document versions will be maintained for the Project Charter and Project Scope Statement. For all other project documents, only the latest version will be saved.

Major changes to the document will result in a new version number (e.g., 2.0, 3.0). Minor changes will result in a new decimal (e.g., 2.1, 2.2).

Communication Management Plan (see pages 124–125)

COMMUNICATION MANAGEMENT PLAN			
Project Name	DCV4Launch–DecoCam V4 Product Launch		
Communication Name	**Description**	**Audience/ Attendees**	**Timing**
Project Kickoff Meeting	Meeting to review the Project Charter for the project and obtain formal approval to proceed to the Planning Phase.	Casey Serrador Arun Singh Sophie Featherstone	Mar 25, 2020
Distribution of the Project Charter	Project Charter sent as email by Sophie Featherstone.	Project Managers of the other V4 projects	Mar 27, 2020
Scope Review and Sign Off Meeting	Meeting to formally review the project plans and obtain approval to proceed to the Executing Phase.	Casey Serrador Arun Singh Project team	Apr 3, 2020
Daily Project Team Huddle	Daily 15-minute meeting of the product launch team to review the current status of the project and outstanding issues.	Project team	Daily, beginning: Apr 6, 2020
Project Status Report	Weekly status report. Email sent by Sophie Featherstone.	Arun Singh Project Managers of the other V4 projects	Weekly: Thursdays by noon
Project Status Review Meeting	Weekly review of all DecoCam V4 projects.	Arun Singh Project Managers of the other V4 projects	Weekly: Fridays at 1:00 p.m.
Company Announcement	An announcement of the new product launch. This information will be included in the Weekly Message Board.	Deco Productions employees	May 8, 2020
Lessons Learned	Meeting to review the lessons of the project in order to improve future projects.	Arun Singh Project team Adrian Binkley	May 11, 2020
Final Project Meeting	Final review of the project's results.	Casey Serrador Arun Singh Project team	May 13, 2020

Quality Assurance Plan (see pages 136–137)

QUALITY ASSURANCE PLAN

Project Name

DCV4Launch–DecoCam V4 Product Launch

Quality Assurance Processes

1. All written materials are verified with the company's standard spelling and grammar checking software.

2. All project deliverables are verified as follows:
   • Test #1: The team member who creates the deliverable will verify that it meets the defined specifications.
   • Test #2: Jason will perform the tests defined in the Test Plan below.

3. Each team member will provide an overview of their recently completed work at the daily team huddle.

Test Plan

Deliverable	Description	Performed By
Trade Show Signage	Test #1	Chris
	Test #2: 1. Spelling/grammar of all text contains no errors. 2. Graphics according to company standards. 3. Information on the banner is accurate (e.g., names, links, dates). 4. Banner stand meets the size requirements.	Jason
Booth Giveaways	Test #1	Chris
	Test #2: 1. Spelling/grammar of all text contains no errors. 2. Graphics according to company standards. 3. Information on the giveaway is accurate (e.g., names, links, dates).	Jason
Multimedia Demo	Test #1	Chris
	Test #2: 1. Multimedia demo instructions contain no spelling/grammar errors. 2. Multimedia demo instructions accurately describe the demo. 3. Repeated use of the demo does not cause dizziness or other physical effects.	Jason

Social Media	Test #1	Sarah
	Test #2: 1. Spelling/grammar of all text contains no errors. 2. All names and titles are correct.	Jason
Website Updates	Test #1	Sarah
	Test #2: 1. Spelling/grammar of all text contains no errors. 2. All names and titles are correct.	Jason
Press Release	Test #1	Sarah
	Test #2: 1. Spelling/grammar of all text contains no errors. 2. Information in the press release is accurate (e.g., names, links, dates). 3. Meets CP style standards	Jason
Promotional Video	Test #1	Maddy
	Test #2: 1. Video is viewable on all major devices. 2. Spelling/grammar of all text contains no errors. 3. Information in the video is accurate (e.g., names, links, dates).	Jason

Issue Log (see page 146)

ISSUE LOG			
Project Name			
DCV4Launch–DecoCam V4 Product Launch			
Issue #	**Description**	**Priority**	**Status**
13	The Deco Productions company logo on the trade show banner is too small.	Medium	Not started
14	The trade show banner stand is not available.	Medium	Not started
15	The price of the giveaways (i.e., the postcards) is 40% more than budgeted. • Chris verified that the original estimate was too low. No further action to be taken.	Low	NPW
16	The demo version from the Development project team is late—these are usually sent as part of the media outreach. • Sophie requested more information from the project manager of the Development project team. Sarah will consider alternatives once this information is received.	Medium	Started
17	The first version of the multimedia demo isn't working as planned—the user experience is not very effective. • Decision made to upgrade the demo software to a newer version. • Chris tested the new version and resolved the issue.	High	Complete
18	The main actor signed for the promotional video was diagnosed with pneumonia and may need to be replaced. • Decision made to hire a new actor. • Maddy is working with the Resource Manager to hire a new actor.	High	Started

Change Request (Postcard) (see pages 149–150)

CHANGE REQUEST FORM	
Project Name	DCV4Launch–DecoCam V4 Product Launch
Requested By	Chris Sandburg
Request Date	April 7, 2020

**Part A. Description of the Requested Change
(Completed by the Requestor)**

Change the trade show giveaways to resemble a picture frame rather than a postcard.

**Part B. Benefit of the Requested Change
(Completed by the Requestor)**

A picture frame would more accurately demonstrate the benefit of the DecoCam software—it would allow the user to take outstanding pictures that would subsequently be framed. A postcard may be confusing as it suggests a travel theme which is unrelated to DecoCam.

**Part C. Impacts to the Project
(Completed by the Project Manager)**

The impacts to the project are as follows:
- No change to the work effort or project schedule.
- The supplier could produce a card that would resemble a picture frame. The unit cost would increase from $1.00 to $1.20. For the 2,000 cards that will be ordered, this results in a $400 budget increase to order the cards.
- No change in the quality.
- No change to the risk.

**Part D. Change Request Decision
(Completed by the Project Change Committee)**

The Project Change Committee approved this request. The picture frame trade show giveaway will be more effective and memorable than the postcard. This benefit outweighed the $400 cost increase.

Change Request (Modified Multimedia Demo) (see page 150)

CHANGE REQUEST FORM	
Project Name	DCV4Launch–DecoCam V4 Product Launch
Requested By	Zoe Purdie
Request Date	April 7, 2020

Part A. Description of the Requested Change (Completed by the Requestor)

Develop a modified version of the DecoCam V4 software to be used in the trade show multimedia demo.

Part B. Benefit of the Requested Change (Completed by the Requestor)

The modified version would have restricted functionality but would allow the user to fully experience the system, rather than using the simulated slideshow application that is currently being planned.

Part C. Impacts to the Project (Completed by the Project Manager)

The impacts to the project are as follows:
- The modified version of the software could be completed for $6,000.
- No change to the project schedule.
- There is an increased risk that the new software contains errors that become evident during the trade show.

Part D. Change Request Decision (Completed by the Project Change Committee)

The Project Change Committee rejected this request. While the potential for this modified software is appealing, the increased cost would cause the project to exceed its $60,000 budget. As well, the increased potential for problems at the trade show is not acceptable.

Project Status Report (see pages 168–169)

PROJECT STATUS REPORT	
Project Name	DCV4Launch–DecoCam V4 Product Launch
For Week Ending	Friday, April 10, 2020
Project Status	Yellow
Status Description	The work of the project is proceeding well, with all tasks currently on schedule. The project is reporting a yellow project status for two main reasons: 1. The project is currently $820 over budget. 2. The first issue listed below (i.e., the need to hire a new video actor) could potentially delay the completion of the promotional video. The source of the budget increase is being investigated—more information to come. A high priority has been placed on acquiring a new actor as soon as possible.

Activities—During the Past Week

Create sign graphics/text.

Order banner stands.

Create holograph cards.

Create social media strategy.

Develop social media content.

Develop video concept.

Develop video storyboard.

Activities—Planned for Next Week

Create holographic cards.

Order cards.

Create mural for booth.

Update product page.

Create online slideshow.

Create outreach list.

Project Issues

The main actor who was signed for the promotional video was recently diagnosed with pneumonia. The decision was made to hire a new actor.

Continued

The demo version from the Development project team is late—this is usually sent as part of the media outreach. More information has been requested from the Development team's project manager.

The Deco Productions company logo on the tradeshow banner is too small. No progress has been made on this issue.

The trade show banner stand selected is not available. No progress has been made on this issue.

Project Changes

The trade show giveaways will be changed to resemble a picture frame rather than a postcard.

Final Project Report (see pages 187–188)

FINAL PROJECT REPORT	
Project Name	DCV4Launch–DecoCam V4 Product Launch
Date Produced	May 13, 2020
Project Sponsor	Arun Singh
Project Manager	Sophie Featherstone
Project Goals	
Project Charter	The goals of the project are to successfully launch DecoCam V4 by the project target dates, within the project budget, and to support the company's goal of a 5% increase in DecoCam's market share.
Actual Results	Target Dates: The project met the target dates (see below for details). Budget: The final project cost was within the updated project budget (see below for details). Market Share: As all objectives were completed, this project supported the company's goals of a 5% increase in market share. The assessment of the market share achieved will become known in the next six months.
Project Objectives	
Project Charter	The objectives of the project are to: • Update the product information on the company website and printed materials. • Promote the new product through existing communication channels. • Create a promotional video. • Create trade show materials.
Actual Results	All of the project objectives were achieved.
Completion Date	
Project Charter	May 8, 2020 (product launch) May 13, 2020 (project complete)
Actual Results	The project is ready to launch by May 7, 2020 (one day early). The project will be closed on May 13, 2020.
Budget	
Project Charter	$60,000
Actual Results	The final costs for the project were $61,250. The original Project Charter budget was increased to $62,600 during the project due to the following approved changes: • Change the trade show giveaways to resemble a picture frame rather than a postcard ($400). • Upgrade the software required to create the Multimedia Demo ($1,600). • Outsource the development of the Multimedia Demo ($600). Based on the modified budget, the project was under budget by $1,350.

Lessons Learned Report (see pages 191–192)

LESSONS LEARNED REPORT	
Project Name	DCV4Launch–DecoCam V4 Product Launch
Project Sponsor	Arun Singh
Project Manager	Sophie Featherstone

What went well during the project?

The project kickoff meeting was very effective. The stakeholders found that it was very informative and they were able to understand the objectives of the project.

The Project Scope Statement contained a useful level of detail and team members found that it was helpful as they completed their tasks during the project.

The duration estimates for the project's activities were accurate. Most activities were completed in the planned duration.

The on-the-job training provided by Maddy to Eli seemed to work well.

The level of risk management seemed to be effective. There were no significant surprises during the project.

What did not go well during the project?

Teams members were not quite sure when their tasks were scheduled. While this information was contained in the project management software, they did not have access to it and were often unsure about the schedule.

The cost estimates for materials seemed to be optimistic—when they were purchased, the prices tended to be higher than estimated. The sales tax also didn't seem to be included in the original estimates.

The team members were not always available when originally planned in the Project HR Requirements spreadsheet. This necessitated that the project schedule be updated numerous times.

There were times during the project when there wasn't enough communication between project team members. This caused problems regarding the project's quality that needed to be addressed later in the project.

A number of problems regarding the project's quality came up at the end of the project. A great deal of work took place to correct the issues.

What should we do differently next time?	How will this be done?
Ensure team members know what their tasks are for each week.	Investigate ways to produce individual weekly task reports for each team member. This will ensure each team member is aware of their tasks.
Improve cost estimating.	Spend additional time validating the material resources estimates through online checks of the supplier websites. Be sure to include the sales tax in the estimate and assume an additional 10% cost to account for possible price increases.

Improve resource estimating and management.	Plan a bi-weekly meeting between the Project Manager and the Resource Manager to ensure the Project HR Requirements spreadsheet remains accurate.
Improve the communication within the project team.	In future projects, ensure that all team members understand that the daily huddle is a mandatory meeting.
Put more focus on project quality.	Once the Quality Assurance Plan is created, hold a team meeting to review the document and provide feedback.

References

Arora, M., & Baronikian, H. (2013). *Leadership in Project Management* (2nd ed.). Leadership Publishing House, Toronto, ON.

AXELOS. (2017). *Managing Successful Projects with Prince2*. TSO, Norwich, England.

Baca, C. M. (2007). *Project Management for Mere Mortals*. Addison-Wesley, Boston, MA.

Barkley, B. T. (2004). *Project Risk Management*. McGraw-Hill, New York, NY.

Barrett, D. J. (2011). *Leadership Communication* (3rd ed.). McGraw-Hill, New York, NY.

Basu, R. (2012). *Managing Quality in Projects*. Gower Publishing Limited, Surrey, England.

Berkun, S. (2005). *The Art of Project Management*. O'Reilly Media Inc., Sebastopol, CA.

Blake, R. R., & Mouton, J. S. (1964). *The Managerial Grid*. Gulf Publishing Company, Houston, TX.

Blanchard, K., Zigarmi, P., & Zigarmi, D. (1985). *Leadership and the One Minute Manager*. William Morrow and Company, Inc., New York, NY.

Campbell, M. (2009). *Communication Skills for Project Managers*. Amacom Books, New York, NY.

Cleland, D. I., & Ireland, L. R. (2006). *Project Management Strategic Design and Implementation* (5th ed.). McGraw-Hill, New York, NY.

Cook, C. R. (2005). *Just Enough Project Management*. McGraw-Hill, New York, NY.

Crosby, B. C., Bryson, J. M., & Anderson, S. R. (2003). *Leadership for the Common Good Fieldbook*. University of Minnesota Extension Service, St. Paul, MN.

Darnall, R. W., & Preston, J. M. (2013). *Project Management from Simple to Complex*. Flat World Knowledge Inc., Washington, DC.

Deming, W. E. (2000). *Out of the Crisis*. The MIT Press, Cambridge, MA.

Dinsmore, P. C., & Cabanis-Brewin, J. (2011). *The AMA Handbook of Project Management* (3rd ed.). Amacom Books, New York, NY.

Eden, C., & Ackermann, F. (1998). *Making Strategy: The Journey of Strategic Management*. Sage Publications Ltd., London, England.

Fleming, Q. W. (2003). *Project Procurement Management: Contracting, Subcontracting, Teaming*. FMC Press, Tustin, CA.

French, J. R. P., & Raven, B. H. (1959). "The Bases of Social Power," in *Studies of Social Power*, ed. D. Cartwright. Institute for Social Research, Ann Arbor, MI.

Garton, E., & Noble, A. (2017, July 19). *How to Make Agile Work for the C-Suite*. Retrieved from www.hbr.org/2017/07/how-to-make-agile-work-for-the-c-suite.

Gido, J., & Clements, J. P. (2009). *Successful Project Management* (5th ed.). South-Western Cengage Learning, Mason, OH.

Goodman, L. J., & Love, R. N. (1980). *Project Planning and Management—An Integrated Approach*. Pergamon Press, New York, NY.

Gross, J. M., & McGinnis, K. R. (2003). *Kanban Made Simple*. Amacon Books, New York, NY.

Handy, C. (1993). *Understanding Organizations*. Penguin Books Ltd., London, England.

Hansen, B. J. (1964). *Practical Pert*. America House, Washington, DC.

Heldman, K. (2005). *Project Manager's Spotlight on Risk Management*. Jossey-Bass, San Francisco, CA.

Hersey, P., Blanchard, K., & Johnson, D. (1996). *Management of Organizational Behaviour: Utilizing Human Resources*. Prentice Hall, Upper Saddle River, NJ.

Hill, G. M. (2010). *The Complete Project Management Methodology and Toolkit*. CRC Press, Boca Raton, FL.

Holpp, L. (1999). *Managing Teams*. McGraw-Hill, New York, NY.

Huemann, M. (2015). *Human Resource Management in the Project-Oriented Organization*. Gower Publishing, Surrey, England.

Hughes, R. L., Ginnett, R. C., & Curphy, G. J. (2014). *Leadership: Enhancing the Lessons of Experience* (8th ed.). McGraw-Hill, New York, NY.

Juran, J. M., & De Feo, J. A. (2010). *Juran's Quality Handbook: The Complete Guide to Performance Excellence.* McGraw-Hill, New York, NY.

Kerzner, H. (2013). *Project Management: A Systems Approach to Planning, Scheduling, and Controlling.* John Wiley & Sons, Inc., Hoboken, NJ.

Klastorin, T. (2004). *Project Management Tools and Trade-Offs.* John Wiley & Sons, Inc., Hoboken, NJ.

Lewis, J. P. (2008). *Mastering Project Management.* McGraw-Hill, New York, NY.

Meredith, J. R., & Mantel, S. J. (2003). *Project Management: A Managerial Approach* (5th ed.). John Wiley & Sons, Inc., Hoboken, NJ.

Munter, M. (1997). *Guide to Managerial Communication* (4th ed.). Prentice Hill, Upper Saddle River, NJ.

Neave, H. R. (1990). *The Deming Dimension.* SPC Press Inc., Knoxville, TN.

Nutt, P. C., & Backoff, R. W. (1992). *Strategic Management of Public and Third Sector Organizations: A Handbook For Leaders.* Jossey-Bass, San Francisco, CA.

Pinto, J. K. (2016). *Project Management: Achieving Competitive Advantage.* Pearson Education, Inc., New York, NY.

Portny, S. E., Mantel, S. J., Meredith, J. R., Shafer, S. M., & Sutton, M. M. (2008). *Project Management: Planning, Scheduling, and Controlling Projects.* John Wiley & Sons, Inc., Hoboken, NJ.

Project Management Institute. (2013). *A Guide to the Project Management Body of Knowledge (PMBOK® Guide)* (5th ed.). Newtown Square, PA.

Rose, K. H. (2005). *Project Quality Management: Why, What and How.* J. Ross Publishing, Boca Raton, FL.

Royer, P. S. (2002). *Project Risk Management: A Proactive Approach.* Management Concepts Inc., Vienna, VA.

Schwaber, K. (2004). *Agile Project Management with Scrum.* Microsoft Press, Redmond, WA.

Shtub, A., Bard, J. F., & Globerson, S. (2005). *Project Management: Processes, Methodologies, and Economics* (2nd ed.). Pearson Inc., Upper Saddle River, NJ.

Smith, K. A. (2014). *Teamwork and Project Management.* McGraw-Hill, New York, NY.

Summers, D. C. S. (2005). *Quality Management.* Pearson Prentice Hall, Upper Saddle River, NJ.

Sutherland, J. (2014). *Scrum—The Art of Doing Twice the Work in Half the Time.* Crown Business, New York, NY.

Sutherland, J., & Schwaber, K. (2016, July). *The Scrum Guide.* Retrieved from www.scrumguides.org/docs/scrumguide/v2016/2016-Scrum-Guide-US.pdf.

Van Vliet, V. (2012). *Henry Gantt.* Retrieved from www.toolshero.com/toolsheroes/henry-gantt.

Yukl, G. A. (2010). *Leadership in Organizations.* Pearson Prentice Hall, Upper Saddle River, NJ.